MW01091912

JAGDPANZER

OSPREY
PUBLISHING

JAGDP

ANZER

Thomas Anderson

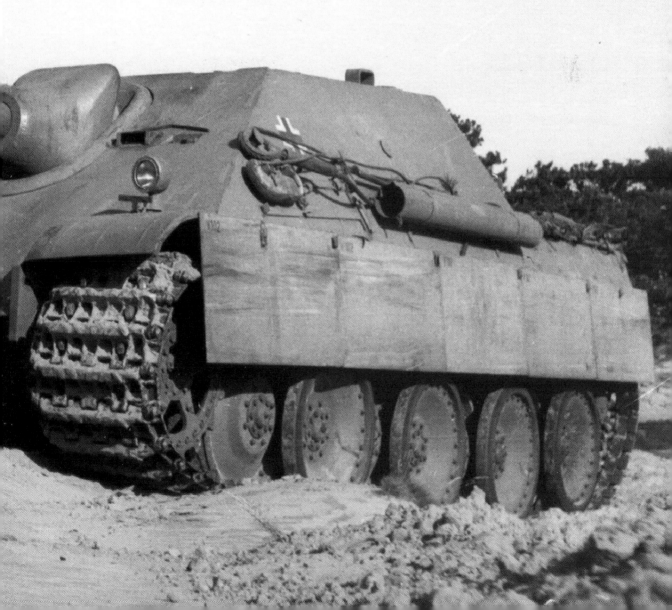

OSPREY PUBLISHING
Bloomsbury Publishing Plc
Kemp House, Chawley Park, Cumnor Hill,
Oxford OX2 9PH, UK
29 Earlsfort Terrace, Dublin 2, Ireland
1385 Broadway, 5th Floor, New York, NY 10018, USA
E-mail: info@ospreypublishing.com
www.ospreypublishing.com

OSPREY is a trademark of Osprey Publishing Ltd

First published in Great Britain in 2024

© Thomas Anderson, 2024

Thomas Anderson has asserted his right under the
Copyright, Designs and Patents Act, 1988, to be identified
as Author of this work.

For legal purposes the Acknowledgements on p. 272
constitute an extension of this copyright page.

All rights reserved. No part of this publication may be
reproduced or transmitted in any form or by any means,
electronic or mechanical, including photocopying,
recording, or any information storage or retrieval system,
without prior permission in writing from the publishers.

A catalogue record for this book is available from the
British Library.

ISBN: HB 9781472857361;
eBook 9781472857378
ePDF 9781472857385
XML 9781472857354

24 25 26 27 28   10 9 8 7 6 5 4 3 2 1

Conceived and edited by Jasper Spencer-Smith
Page Layout: Crispin Goodall
Jacket design: Stewart Larking
Index: Michael Napier
Produced for Bloomsbury Publishing Plc
by Editworks Limited

Unless otherwise stated, all images are from the author's
collection.
Printed and bound in India by Replika Press Private Ltd.
Osprey Publishing supports the Woodland Trust, the UK's
leading woodland conservation charity.

To find out more about our authors and books visit www.
ospreypublishing.com. Here you will find extracts, author
interviews, details of forthcoming events and the option
to sign up for our newsletter.

CONTENTS

Introduction

The introduction and large-scale use of tanks by Great Britain and France in World War I changed the nature of warfare significantly.

Despite their numerous mechanical shortcomings, the first tanks proved more than capable of breaking through enemy lines that previously had been frozen in the stalemate of static trench warfare, giving the Allied forces a new momentum. Thanks to their effective tactical capabilities, these new weapons were to find a permanent place in the inventories of many armies around the world after the end of the war.

Whereas Great Britain and France had begun developing their individual machines in 1915, Germany only recognized the combat value of the type after the first massed deployment of British tanks on 16 September 1916. The German Army had dramatically underestimated the capabilities of these machines, and even after the initial surprise had been overcome, it still proved incapable of adapting sufficiently quickly to the changed situation. Consequently, German tank development and production did not begin until 1917 and the first A7V appeared on the battlefront in early 1918.

The basic characteristics of the new weapon, namely armour protection, firepower and mobility, were still at a very rudimentary stage of development, and the technology of the day was prone to failure. The tank provided a certain degree of cross-country mobility, but this was ultimately limited because of the extremely difficult terrain of the Western Front. Furthermore, the mechanical components – engine, transmission and steering gear – were not sufficiently reliable.

The riveted armour plating of the vehicles was secure against fire from 7.92mm infantry weapons but could, however, be penetrated by concentrated machine-gun fire or shrapnel.

Opposite: The German Reich was late in developing a tank, resulting in some 20 of the A7V being built by end of World War I. However, a large number of *Buetepanzer* (captured tanks) – mainly British – were recovered from the battlefront and, where possible, repaired and used by German forces. (NARA)

The French-built Renault FT was the first tank to have the main gun, a 37mm Puteaux SA 1918, mounted in a rotatable turret. The vehicle is in service with the reconnaissance section in the 7th Battalion, First Canadian Division, Canadian Expeditionary Force. (NARA)

The Rhomboid-shaped British tanks carried their armament in large sponsons on each side, and a large proportion, known as 'females', were armed with four 0.303-inch Vickers machine guns (MG) and a secondary Hotchkiss. In contrast, the 'male' vehicles had a 57mm Hotchkiss quick-firning 6-Pounder (QF 6-Pdr) cannon mounted in each sponson and three 0.303in Hotchkiss MG as secondary armament. The machine guns could effectively engage enemy infantry and successfully pin them down, while tanks fitted with cannons were able to safely take out artillery and weapons in bunkers.

The French finally installed the 75mm *Canon de 75 modéle* 1897 in the St Chamond, and this exceptionally successful field gun offered a very wide range of uses. It would be 1939 before a comparable gun was mounted in

a tank: the Soviet-built Kliment Voroshilov-1 (KV-1), and later the T-34. Ironically, a large number of these guns, captured from the French Army in 1940, would be used by German anti-tank forces in 1943.

In the course of the first missions by tanks, both the British and the French were to adapt their concepts to the changing conditions in battle. The first special variants were also produced to fulfil specific tactical tasks. In this way, light and medium tanks (Whippet and Renault FT) with improved tactical mobility emerged over time and, due to their higher speed, exploited a breakthrough and caused havoc behind enemy lines.

The Renault-built FT, often called FT 17, also introduced another revolutionary feature: the main armament, an 8mm Hotchkiss *modéle* 1914 machine gun or alternatively a 37mm Puteaux SA 1918 gun, was mounted in a rotatable turret. Now the weapon could be quickly traversed to engage

The British army used large numbers of medium tanks during World War I. The Mark 1, was armed with two Ordnance Quick-Firing (OQF) 6-Pdr guns. The rear-mounted steering aid was not used on later versions. The wire-covered frame, over the superstructure, was to prevent hand grenades landing on the thin steel roof.

The St Chamond was one of the first tanks developed by France. The type utilized Holt-type suspension on a chassis too short for the large superstructure. This resulted in long front and rear overhangs which compromised off-road mobility, but the vehicle was well-armed with a powerful 75mm *Canon de 75 modéle* 1897. (NARA)

new targets without changing the direction of the tank. In addition to saving time, it also meant that the vulnerable drive and steering were used less. On the German side, the realization of this existential danger for the front-line troops naturally led to the development of suitable defensive weapons. At first, existing light field guns and howitzers – horse-drawn artillery – were used to reinforce or defend vulnerable sections of terrain. Used correctly, these proved to be quite effective in neutralizing the attacking tanks.

The main burden of fighting the British and French tanks, however, lay with the German front-line soldier, who had to attack these armoured monsters with inadequate weapons in close combat.

In the period before World War II, the German army built up its anti-tank force as the initial equipment of 3.7cm guns was successively replaced by more powerful weapons as a result of developments that became apparent as early as 1940. In 1941, the 5cm *Panzerabwehrkanone* (PaK – anti-tank gun) 38 was the standard weapon, and a year later the 7.5cm PaK 40 was introduced. This rapid development documented the change of the *Panzerabwehrtruppe* (PzAbwTrp – tank defence force) from a defensive force into an offensive weapon. Reflecting this change of emphasis, the designation was changed to

The Medium Mark A Whippet gave British forces a tank which, due to it being a little faster, was intended to support an infantry advance after heavy tanks had penetrated enemy lines. Consequently, the vehicle was fabricated from 14mm armour and armed with four 7.7mm Hotchkiss machine guns. (NARA)

Panzerjägertruppe (PzJgTrp – tank hunter force). In response to the increasing challenges in the Soviet Union and in the deserts of North Africa, the mobility of the tank destroyer units was also improved during 1942. In order to meet the needs of modern warfare, the existing weapons, such as captured Russian guns and the 7.5cm PaK 40, were mounted on a tank chassis as a *Selbstfahrlafette* (Sf – self-propelled) gun.

Finally, another turning point occurred during 1943. Due to the success of assault guns, which had been armed with a 7.5cm *Langrohr* (*lang* – long -barrel) gun since the beginning of 1942, increasing numbers of the type were now being issued to tank destroyer units. These turretless vehicles were to make history, especially on the Eastern Front. Operating in support of the hard-pressed infantry, who had long been calling for fully armoured support vehicles, they soon became indispensable. One year later, in 1944, the ultimate development in Germany came when the first *Jagdpanzer* (JgdPz – hunting tank) was issued to the *Panzerjäger* (PzJg – tank hunter) units.

A column of Medium Mark A Whippet tanks from the 3rd Tank Brigade, 3rd Battalion (Light), Tank Corps, pass men of a New Zealand infantry division near Mailly-Maillet, during the German spring offensive which commenced on 28 March 1918. (NARA)

Anti-tank Defences: 1935–1939

1

With the re-establishment or declaration of German military sovereignty in 1935, the German armed forces were to be renamed in their entirety. The former *Reichsheer* now became the *Wehrmacht.*

During the build-up of the *Wehrmacht*, significant efforts were made to motorize the army. However, limited resources, and a means of production which was not yet fully developed, allowed only for a slow implementation of this equipment.

During World War I, it had been decided to introduce a relatively light 3.7cm anti-tank gun. At the time, this seemed effective enough to penetrate the weak armour of most contemporary tanks. The decision was also based on the need to keep the combat weight of the weapon low so that a team of few soldiers could easily move it in the field. Thus, on the German side, this 3.7cm *Tank-Abwehr-Kanone* (TaK – anti-tank gun) was introduced. A gun of this class was to become the standard anti-tank weapon after World War I.

Even in *Reichswehr* times, the equipment issued to the anti-tank units was given high priority.

Internationally, anti-tank units initially used weapons ranging from 20mm to 47mm. It should also be remembered that the armies of Great Britain, France, the USA and the Soviet Union kept large quantities of 75mm and 76.2mm field guns in their divisional artillery which, thanks to their ballistic performance (sufficiently high muzzle velocity) and their relatively low weight, could, at least in theory, also be used to fight tanks.

Germany chose a different path. The artillery regiments of the tank and infantry divisions were to be equipped with the 10.5cm *leichte Feldhaubitz* (le FH – light field howitzer) 18, in addition to the 15cm *schwere Feldhaubitz* (s FH – heavy field howitzer) 18 or 10cm *Kanone* (K – cannon) 18. This latter had a remarkable effect on the target but was only marginally suitable for fighting

Opposite: German tank destroyer forces were initially equipped with the 3.7cm *Panzerabwehrkanone* (PaK – anti-tank gun). Here, a gun team demonstrate the weapon during a propaganda rally organized by the *Reichsparteitag* (Reich Party Congress) at Nuremberg in 1936. (Getty)

The 5cm PaK 38 L/60 was designed and developed by Rheinmetall-Borsig in 1938, but entered service too late for the invasion of France. However, the weapon was in front-line service for *Uternehmen* (Operation) *Barbarossa* but was found to be ineffective against the Soviet-built T-34 medium and KV heavy tanks.

tanks. In 1941, when the well-armoured Red Army T-34 medium and KV heavy tanks were encountered, the lack of a 75mm gun became painfully apparent.

3.7cm PaK

Development of a 3.7cm PaK commenced in 1925 and the gun was introduced into service in 1928. Initially horse-drawn, the gun was mounted on a flat, split-trail, two-wheeled carriage fitted with bullet-proof tyres. The cradle also housed the recoil and recuperator system. A small, 5-mm thick sloping shield protected the crew against infantry fire and shell splinters. A basic requirement was to keep the weight of the gun as low as possible so that it could be easily turned and moved over short distances by the crew. In 1934, it was decided to convert the type for motorized traction. The 3.7cm PaK was introduced as the standard weapon of the *Panzerabwehr-Kompanien* (PzAbwKp – anti-tank companies). By 1939, more than 10,000 weapons of the type had been delivered.

4.7cm PaK (Böhler)

In the mid-1930s, the Austrian manufacturer Böhler had developed a 4.7cm gun that was intended to meet the specific requirements of the Austrian army.

The gun was easy to dismantle so that it could be deployable in the mountains. After the wheels were removed, the gun had a very low profile. Licences to produce the weapon were sold to Italy and a number of other nations.

When Austria was annexed by the German Reich, 330 of these guns were commandeered. Although the armour penetration performance of the 4.7cm PaK(ö) – the 'ö' indicates *Osterreich* (Austria) origin – exceeded that of the 3.7cm PaK, these weapon was not initially adopted by the German field army, possibly because the introduction of the more powerful 5cm PaK 38 was planned for 1940. Instead, the existing 4.7cm PaK(ö) were initially installed in the Siegfried Line (Westwall) fortifications, allowing the 3.7cm PaK which it replaced to be redeployed into the anti-tank companies.

During the war, Italian-manufactured Böhler guns (*Canone da* 47/32) continued to be used by German units whenever available.

3.7cm PaK(t)

When Czechoslovakia was annexed, two types of anti-tank weapons fell into German hands.

The 3.7cm PUV vz 37 was a gun of conventional design that was broadly comparable to the German 3.7cm PaK in terms of ballistic performance. The gun was introduced, as was the 3.7cm PaK 37(t) – the '(t)' indicates

A squad of *Fallschirmjäger* (paratroopers) manhandle a 4.2cm PaK 41 anti-tank gun into a concealed firing position. The gun barrel was designed by using the Gerlich taper-bore principle and fired hard-core ammunition which could penetrate 100mm at a range of 100m.

Although the SdKfz 10 was the smallest German half-track vehicle, it was highly mobile and had excellent cross-country performance. The type had a towing capacity of 1,000kg, which made it ideal as a tractor for towing light artillery and anti-tank guns. But the vehicle was complicated to produce, which meant that supply would never meet the numbers required on the battlefront.

Tschechoslowakisch (Czechoslovak) origin – in the anti-tank companies in some infantry divisions.

The armament statistics kept by the *Heereswaffenamt* (HWa – army weapons office) reported a stock of 1,205 guns in April 1940.

4.7cm PaK(t)

Another weapon found at Škoda in 1938 was the 4.7cm PUV vz 36 anti-tank gun. Due to its performance, which was clearly superior to that of the German 3.7cm PaK, the gun was initially adopted as the 4.7cm PaK(t).

Initially, only 36 of the type were available in April 1940, but from November onwards, for an unknown reason, the HWa changed the designation and counting method. Subsequently, the number of guns now called 4.7cm PaK 36(t) jumped to 452; an explanation for this anomaly cannot be given.

This gun was to be used to create the first self-propelled anti-tank gun. For this purpose, the *Panzerkampfwagen* (PzKpfw – tank) I, *Ausführung* (Ausf – model/mark) B was fitted with a simple armoured superstructure with the

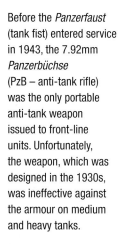

Before the *Panzerfaust* (tank fist) entered service in 1943, the 7.92mm *Panzerbüchse* (PzB – anti-tank rifle) was the only portable anti-tank weapon issued to front-line units. Unfortunately, the weapon, which was designed in the 1930s, was ineffective against the armour on medium and heavy tanks.

The solid rubber tyres fitted on the carriage of the 5cm PaK 38 were safe against fire from light infantry weapons, but due to their narrow section, the gun easily sank into soft ground.

The 4.2cm PaK 41 entered service between January and August 1942, with the majority of the 150 produced being issued to *Luftwaffe* field units. In combat, use was somewhat affected, since the weapon was designed to fire tungsten-type ammunition and this was always in short supply.

Performance Data of Pre-War Anti-tank Guns

Guns are identified by the following numerals:

1 = 3.7cm PaK
2 = 4.7cm PaK K36(t)(*)
3 = Canon de 25mm mle 34
4 = Canon de 47mm mle 37
5 = Ordnance Quick-Firing (QF) 2-pdr
6 = 37mm M 1930 (**)
7 = 45mm M 1937

Weapon	1	2 (*)	3	4	5	6 (**)	7
Origin	German	German	French	French	British	Soviet	Soviet
Calibre	3.7cm	4.7cm	25mm	47mm	40mm	37mm	47mm
Barrel	1,665mm	2,040mm	1,600mm	2,491mm	2,000mm	1,665mm	2,070mm
Calibre (Length)	L/45	L/43.4	L/64	L/53	L/50	L/45	L/46
Muzzle Velocity (***)	780mps	775mps	920mps	855mps	792mps	780mps	760mps
Range	6,000m	5,200m	n/a	6,500m	7,300m	6,000m	4,400m
Penetration (***) (Range)							
100m	35mm	n/a	35mm	65mm	50mm	35mm	42mm
500m	29mm	50mm	29mm	50mm	45mm	29mm	35mm
1,000m	22mm	n/a	20mm	37mm	35mm	22mm	28mm
1,500m	20mm	n/a	n/a	n/a	30mm	20mm	23mm

(*) Captured weapon from Czechoslovak stock/production
(**) Licensed production of German Rheinmetall-Borsig 3.7cm PaK(1)
(***) Firing standard armour-piercing (AP) round

4.7cm gun mounted centrally on a crossbeam over the fighting compartment. A total of approximately 200 of the type were produced on the light tank chassis.

Tractors

For the successful deployment of the anti-tank weapons, powerful all-terrain towing vehicles were essential. With the beginning of the motorization of the

Above: The 3.7cm PaK was the standard weapon of the German tank destroyer battalion until the end of 1941. Originally, it was designed to penetrate armour up to 30mm thick, but by 1939 it was almost obsolete. (Getty)

Left: When the 5cm PaK 38 entered service, German military planners intended it to be towed by a half-track tractor; these were never available in sufficient numbers: a problem which would plague German armoured and artillery units throughout the war.

After the capitulation of France, a vast amount of serviceable equipment became available to German forces. In addition to countless wheeled types, there were also tanks, tracked and half-track vehicles. A large number of Renault UE *Chenilette* (caterpillar) were issued to German artillery units as tractors for light and medium guns.

Wehrmacht in 1935, only commercially available or basically militarized heavy passenger cars were available. However, these types were not at all satisfactory, since all the vehicles had limited load-carrying and towing capacities. Off-road performance was also insufficient, since they lacked all-wheel drive.

From 1938 onwards, the *Panzerabwehr-Abteilungen* (PzAbwAbt – tank destroyer battalions) of the Panzer divisions (PzDiv – tank divisions) were preferentially equipped with the Krupp Kfz 69 Protzkraftwagen, whereas the infantry divisions received basically militarized Kfz 12 medium off-road vehicles.

The powerful *Sonderkraftfahrzeug* (SdKfz – special purpose vehicle) 10, *leichter Zugkraftwagen* (le ZgKw – light half-track tractor), had good performance on and off road. The type and deployment of this equipment was always dependent firstly on the ability of industry to supply and secondly on the location of the front-line units. In short, German industry was never able to supply specialized, standardized towing vehicles in the necessary numbers, so any available vehicles had to be used. In practice, there were correspondingly large deviations from the planned stock targets. In order to meet the

demand, exceptionally large numbers of captured British and French vehicles, commandeered by the *Wehrmacht* in 1941, were used.

Demand for Mobility

As early as the mid-1930s, demands were made to equip not only the tank units but also the anti-tank units with significantly higher mobility and, if possible, with armour protection.

Based on the powerful German half-track tractors, prototypes were developed that carried both a 3.7cm PaK L/70 and a 7.5cm *Feldkanone* (FK – field gun) 16 L/40.8 in a rotatable turret. However, these imaginative state-of-the-art solutions were never introduced; presumably the realization of these plans exceeded the capabilities of the industry.

It is possible that the 7.5cm FK 16 could have given the ground troops of the *Wehrmacht* a clear weapons superiority in 1940. Installation of this weapon in the PzKpfw IV would also have given the *Panzertruppe* the tools to success-fully combat the Russian KV and T-34 tanks that appeared in 1941.

The 2.8cm PaK 41 was also fitted with a taper-bore gun barrel, which reduced from 2.8cm to 20mm. The comparatively light weapon had a good performance; 60mm-thick armour could be penetrated at a range of 100m. The tactical mark is for a special unit which operated behind enemy lines.

Panzerabwehr to Panzerjäger | 2

By the beginning of World War II, most German combat units were equipped with anti-tank units according to plan.

The typical PzDiv had a total of 54 3.7cm PaK. The divisional *Panzerabwehr-Abteilung* (PzAbwAbt – anti-tank battalion) had 36, and their *Schützen-Regiment* (rifle regiment) received 18. In addition, all were issued with an unknown number of light anti-tank weapons such as the *Panzerbüchse* (PzB – anti-tank rifle).

Infantry divisions had a PzAbwAbt of identical strength (36 3.7cm PaK). The infantry regiment had a total of another 36 3.7cm PaK at its disposal. All the *leichte Divisonen* (leDiv – light divisions) and *Gebirgs-Divisionen* (GebDiv – mountain divisions) were similarly equipped.

During the first wartime operations, the organization of the anti-tank units – both as divisional PzAbwAbt and within the companies subordinated to the battalions – was to prove effective. The number of anti-tank guns in the front ranks of the infantry companies was regarded to be sufficient.

However, even before the war, the first doubts arose as to whether the performance of the 3.7cm PaK would be sufficient for future conflicts. The *Fremde Heere: West* (foreign armies: West) had identified new tanks in the French arsenals (Renault R-35, Somua S-35) that were thought to be impervious to fire from the 3.7cm weapon. This assumption was proved correct in 1940.

In parallel to the creation of the anti-tank defence, the *Panzertruppe* (PzTrp – tank force) were also strengthened was decided at an early stage to initially equip these new units with the PzKpfw I light tank. These vehicles were easily procurable, but with their weak armour and two 7.92mm *Maschinengewehr* (MG – machine gun) 34 armament, they had only a modest combat value.

Opposite: Shortly before *Fall Gelb* (Plan Yellow) – the *Blitzkrieg* (lightning) invasion of France – the *Panzerjäger* (PzJg – tank hunter) I, built on the chassis of a PzKpfw I Ausf B, entered service with German *Panzerabwehr-Truppe* (tank destroyer units). The type was more mobile than a conventional towed gun and mounted a powerful Czech-built 4.7cm anti-tank cannon.

The later PzDiv were equipped with two powerful types. The *Zugführerwagen* (ZW – platoon commander's vehicle), later the PzKpfw III, was equipped with a 3.7cm weapon like the tank destroyers. The *Begleitwagen* (BW – battalion commander's vehicle), later the PzKpfw IV, carried a 7.5cm *Kampfwagenkanone* (KwK – tank gun) L/24, similar to the weapon that was used as a towed infantry gun by the heavy companies of the rifle or infantry regiments. However, German industry lacked the manufacturing capacity

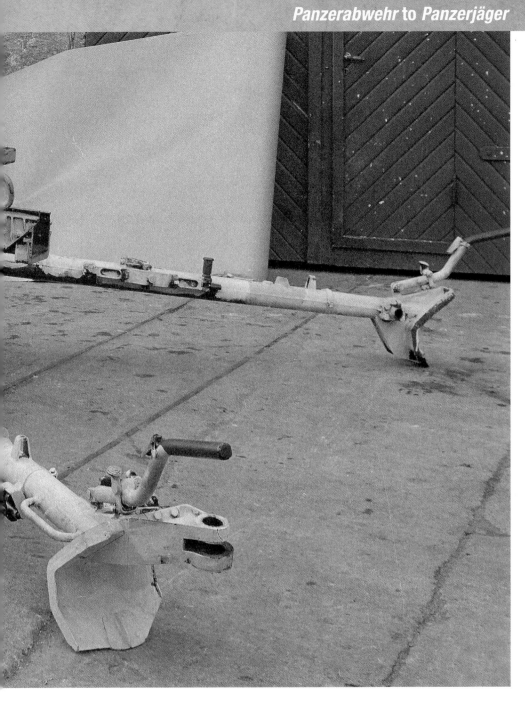

Although the 5cm PaK 38 had respectable ballistic performance, it was soon outclassed. The movement towards significantly better armoured tanks, that began in 1940, was not foreseen by German military planners. Consequently, it was not until mid-1942 that the necessary number of 7.5cm PaK 40 had been issued to front-line anti-tank units.

to produce required numbers of these tanks, so the ambitious plans could not be realized within the intended time frame. Consequently, the PzKpfw I continued to be used until 1940. Additionally, production began in 1936 of a 'gap filler', the PzKpfw II light tank which was armed with a 2cm KwK 30 and a 7.92mm MG 34.

In the procurement of the PzKpfw III and PzKpfw IV, a solution of remarkable economy was found that simplified training, maintenance and

The stationary use of 8.8cm FlaK 18, or another heavy artillery gun, was hazardous since a rapid change of position was impossible if it was located by enemy artillery. As a result, many guns and men were lost.

German commanders on the battlefront often had to deploy their 8.8cm FlaK guns to defend against the well-armoured Red Army tanks. Both the T-34 and KV could be effectively engaged and defeated at ranges over 2,000m.

repair, as well as the supply of ammunition. The battle against France quickly proved the inadequacy of the 3.7cm gun; its poor penetration performance, even when firing 3.7cm *Panzergranate* (PzGr – armour-piercing hard-core ammunition) 40, could only be compensated for by superior German combat tactics.

The 3.7cm PaK was popular with the troops because of its high tactical mobility; after the introduction of explosive grenades, the range of applications of the weapons increased and a multitude of other targets could be successfully engaged. Nevertheless, it was obvious that the PzKpfw III Ausf A to Ausf E (and also the PzKpfw 35(t) and PzKpfw 38(t) used by the *Panzertruppe* since the annexation of Czechoslovakia), like the 3.7cm PaK, were no longer suitable for fighting enemy tanks of the day.

Even before the war began, Rheinmetall-Borsig was working on a superior 5cm anti-tank weapon. This was gradually supplied to the troops in mid-1940, initially in small numbers, and the *Panzerjäger-Abteilungen* (PzJgAbt – tank hunter battalion) – formerly *Panzerabwehr-Abteilungen* (PzAbwAbt) – in the PzDiv were given priority.

The 5cm PaK 38 had a calibre length of L/60 and shared the proven design features of the 3.7cm PaK. Firing height and total weight could be kept low, but the ballistic performance was good and more than sufficient to fight the contemporary French and British tanks.

Both Great Britain and France were lagging behind in development of new weapons, but the latter had introduced a more powerful anti-tank gun at the beginning of the war: the 47mm *Canon de Semi-Automatique modèle* 1937. The performance of this weapon was almost equivalent to that of the 5cm PaK. Many of those captured in the battle were used by the German infantry divisions as the 4.7cn PaK 181(f) – the '(f)' indicates *Frankreich* (France) origin. British forces were less well equipped and continued to rely on the Ordnance Quick Firing (OQF) 2-Pdr until the end of 1941.

When examining the development of anti-tank weapons, a discrepancy emerges that is difficult to explain. Germany was very hesitant to introduce a 7.5cm weapon, although the existence of heavy tanks on the enemy side eventually forced it to do so.

It is possible that Germany modelled the development of anti-tank weapons against its own tanks before the outbreak of the war when heavy tanks with thicker armour were not available. Guderian believed that his vision of highly mobile armoured units was more achievable with armoured vehicles in the 15,000kg to 20,000kg class. The armour of these pre-war types (PzKpfw III and PzKpfw IV) had a thickness of 30mm, and naturally influenced the development of German anti-tank weapons. Basically, the course of the *Blitzkrieg* (lightning war) confirmed Guderian's vision to be correct.

After the conclusion of the French campaign, the PzKpfw III was to be re-armed with the 5cm KwK L/42 gun, but the conversion was slow and the new gun was some 20 percent less powerful than the long-barrel 5cm PaK 38. The HWa, as the responsible agency, cited technical reasons that prevented the installation of the longer and more effective L/60 weapon in the turret, but German industry was not able to solve the installation problems until the end of 1941. Finally, the 5cm KwK L/60 made the PzKpfw III the most important German battle tank at that time and more effective in combat.

But as in France before, the harsh reality of the fighting in the Soviet Union was to show that the PzKpfw III Ausf J, despite its improved main armament, no longer met the requirements of the battlefront. Unnoticed by the world, and especially by German foreign intelligence, the supposedly backward Soviet Union was able to develop two modern tank types before the outbreak of war, each of which had to be considered revolutionary in its own right.

The Soviet-built T-34 medium tank had all-round 45mm-thick sloping armour. Also, it was fitted with simple, but effective, Christie-type suspension with large running wheels and wide plate-type tracks which prevented it from

Opposite: After German anti-tank rifles had proved ineffective, the *Gewehr-Granatgerät* (rifle grenade weapon) was introduced for close combat. The device, which fitted on a standard 7.92mm infantry weapon, fired an explosive grenade or a hollow-charge projectile.

In 1942, close-combat teams began to be issued with the magnetically attached *Hafthohlladung* (Hl – adhesive charge) 3. When carefully placed on the side or rear of an enemy tank, the explosive effect was generally devastating. The paratrooper also carries a 7.92mm *Maschinenpistole* (MP – submachine gun) 40.

sinking into mud or deep snow. Powered by a 500hp diesel engine, the tank had unusually high off-road mobility.

The KV-1 heavy tank, on the other hand, was outstandingly well armoured. In contrast to the T-34, the superstructure was vertically faced and fabricated entirely from 75mm plates. The vehicle was fitted with the same diesel engine as the T-34, but with power slightly increased to 550hp.

Another common feature was the armament, both tanks mounted the 76.2mm Machanov L/30 gun. But in early 1941, this was replaced by the improved 76.2mm F-34, which had good penetration performance due to its better calibre length of L/41.

In the sum of their characteristics, both tanks were far superior to all German tanks on the battlefield. However, both types had serious weaknesses: poor visibility from inside the tank, the lack of radio equipment and poorly designed suspension for the running wheels.

The tank destroyer troops faced comparable problems. The 3.7cm PaK was completely outclassed, even when firing *Panzer-Granate* (PzGr – tungsten core ammunition) 40 the armour of the T-34 and KV-1 could not

German field engineers were issued with a number of close combat weapons for fighting tanks. The *Fallschirmjäger* (paratrooper) on the left holds a *geballte Ladung* (concentrated load) of four 1kg *Sprengbüchse* (high-explosive charge) 24, bundled together with wire. The trooper to the right carries an anti-tank T-mine 35.

be penetrated, even at close range. In individual cases, battle-hardened crews were able to damage the vision devices or parts of the running gear at close range, which could immobilize the tank. While the 5cm PaK38 was more readily available by the end of 1941, even this weapon was no match against the two Soviet types. The troops urgently needed a superior weapon.

Early SP Anti-tank Guns

The infantry and tank units had already complained about the lack of mobility of the tank destroyer guns in the first days of the war. The situation was to worsen with the launch of the Russian campaign; the bottomless mud of the *Rasputitsa* (mud season) made progress almost impossible. The troops were forced to resort to in-the-field solutions. Light and medium anti-tank guns were mounted directly on the towing vehicles (Krupp Protzkraftwagen, Renault UE *Beuteschlepper* [captured tractor], and the SdKfz 10 light half-track tractor). These measures proved quite effective, but the extra weight frequently caused running gear to fail, which soon led to major breakdowns that often overwhelmed field engineer units.

The basic problem had been known to the HWa for a long time. But despite the tight production situation, the first self-propelled gun was built in 1939/40.

A StuG Ausf A next to a PzKpfw IV Ausf C in 1940. Both are armed with the 7.5cm K L/24 or KwK L/24. During the invasion of the Soviet Union, the assault guns were to prove effective in combat against the Russian tanks.

The 4.7cm PaK(t) was mounted on the chassis of the PzKpfw I and fitted with a light armour superstructure. These guns were assigned to some independent PzJgAbt at army troop level from 1940 onwards. By early 1941, the following PzDiv 521, PzDiv 529, PzDiv 605, PzDiv 616, PzDiv 643 and PzDiv 670 were equipped with two or three companies of 4.7cm PaK(t) on PzJg I (a total of 18 and 27 vehicles, respectively). The Leibstandarte SS Adolf Hitler was the only division to receive an integrated company with nine of the type.

In 1941, a similar solution was developed on the chassis of the Renault R-35. These vehicles were also assigned to PzJgAbt 559, PzJgAbt 561 and PzJgAbt 611, independent tank destroyer battalions.

These simple solutions proved to be effective in many tactical situations. However, the Russian winter of 1940–41 temporarily led to the failure of all self-propelled guns, especially the 4.7cm PaK(t) on the R-35, which suffered from severe mechanical problems in the cold weather.

Strong nerves were required to use the *Hafthohlladung* 3. Close-combat teams hid in their foxholes and allowed enemy tanks to pass before leaping out to attach the weapon, which had a four-to-seven-second delay, directly on the side of the hull or turret.

Fifteen 1kg *Sprengbüchsen* were mounted on a board to form a *gestreckte Ladung* (stretched charge). Close-combat teams would attempt to place it under an enemy tank where it would detonate.

Even before the war began, the heavy 8.8cm *Flugzeugabwehrkanone* (FlaK – anti-aircraft gun) 36 was to be built as a *Schartenbrecher* (bunker buster) on the chassis of the SdKfz 8 heavy half-track tractor. These self-propelled guns were initially intended to break through the Maginot Line and other similar fortified defences. However, due to the FlaK 36 having a high muzzle velocity and the resulting accuracy, the weapon was also well suited to combat heavily armoured fighting vehicles.

Ten of these vehicles were built and assigned to PzJgAbt 8. In France, this unit was attached to the 1.PzDiv and 2.PzDiv. After the bunkers of the Maginot Line were overcome unexpectedly quickly, the self-propelled guns were ordered to engage French heavy tanks. During the Russian campaign, PzJgAbt 8 was deployed for anti-tank operations. The 8.8cm FlaK 36 on SdKfz 8 was an effective front-line weapon, but plans to produce a variant mounting a 10.5cm FlaK 39 were not pursued further.

Conversion to 7.5cm

In addition to the PzKpfw III, the PzKpfw IV was available to the *Panzertruppe*. This vehicle was primarily used for direct fire support during a tank attack. For this purpose, the tank mounted the 7.5cm KwK L/24, which was most effective when firing 7.5cm *Granate* (Gr – high-explosive [HE]) 34 ammunition. In an emergency, the 7.5cm *Kopfgranate* (rot) (KGr rot – armour-piercing [AP] shell [red]) could be used to engage enemy tanks. Due to the low muzzle velocity of only 385mps, such an operation was not promising against the modern Russian types with their effective armour.

In 1940, parallel to the initial equipment of the armoured troops, a turretless vehicle was introduced for direct support of the infantry. These vehicles, called *Sturmgeschütz* (StuG – assault gun), were basically part of the artillery. The type was based on the chassis of the PzKpfw III, but with heavier front armour. The main armament was a slightly modified assault gun version of the gun mounted in the PzKpfw IV.

Initially used only at army troop level, assault guns were initially grouped

In the summer of 1942, assault gun units began to be issued with StuG mounting the long-barrelled 7.5cm StuK 40 L/43 or 7.5cm StuK L/48. Although designated as assault guns, both were able to defeat all Red Army tanks at over 1,500m range.

The 5cm PaK 38 was an effective anti-tank gun but it was fitted with narrow-section wheels, which made it difficult to manoeuvre over muddy ground, even when towed by an SdKfz 10/1, light half-track tractor. (Getty)

In spring 1942, front-line units began to be issued with the PzKpfw III Ausf M armed with a 5cm KwK L/60. An experienced commander aware of the gun's limitations, could fight both the T-34 and the KV.

in batteries of six vehicles, then as detachments of three batteries (18 StuG). Despite the obvious disadvantage due to the lack of a turret, the assault guns proved so successful in France that production was quickly increased. At the beginning of the Russian campaign, some 200 StuG were available, compared with 259 PzKpfw III, some 550 PzKpfw 35(t) and PzKpfw 38(t), which were also equipped with a 3.7cm KwK, and approximately 450 PzKpfw IV.

Used offensively with clever tactics, the vehicles were capable of neutralizing even a T-34 or KV-1 at close range with tank or high-explosive ammunition. The projectiles could cause terminal damage to the running or damage the turret ring and gun sleeve. To a certain extent, this was also true for the PzKpfw IV. However, it must be clear that the T-34 and KV-1 could effectively open fire at a much longer range. All German tanks were clearly at a disadvantage.

In view of this fact, the HWa ordered in autumn 1941 that new tanks be developed as quickly as possible, which within a short time would achieve clear and lasting superiority. At the same time, work on a new 7.5cm weapon was intensified. At the beginning of 1942, the 7.5cm KwK 40 was finally ready for service, more than two years after the Red Army had introduced a similar weapon.

The 7.5cm KwK 40 was installed in the PzKpfw IV, the almost identical 7.5cm *Sturmkanone* (StuK – assault cannon) 40 in the StuG. The gun initially

had a calibre length of 3,218mm (L/43). Although this was to be increased to 3,600mm (L/48) in 1943, the ballistic data remained practically unchanged.

The following types of ammunition were available:

- 7.5cm SprGr 34
- 7.5cm PzGr 39
- 7.5cm PzGr 40
- 7.5cm Gr 38

With this weapon, a certain superiority was finally achieved in 1942, not least because of the effective ammunition, which made it possible to fight the both the T-34 and KV-1 at longer ranges. The superiority was even clearer when fighting British and US types in the deserts of North Africa.

New SP Guns

In spring 1942, the tank destroyer troops could finally be equipped with more powerful vehicles. Parallel to the 7.5cm KwK 40, the development of a new anti-tank gun, the 7.5cm PaK 40, was also completed. The introduction was initially slow due to the known production capacity problems in the German armaments industry.

For this reason, captured guns of French or Soviet origin were also issued to

In 1942, the heavy PaK programme was initiated, seeing more than 2,000 of the 7.5cm PaK 97/38 produced. The weapon utilized the barrel of a French-built 75mm field gun, which was mounted on the carriage of a 5cm PaK 38: another indication of the lack of capability of German industry.

The introduction into service of the 7.5cm PaK 40(t) finally gave the PzJg a gun capable of defeating all enemy tanks. The weapon had the same ballistic performance as the 7.5cm KwK and 7.5cm StuK 40.

front-line forces. During the first months of *Unternehmen Barbarossa*, advancing German units were able to capture a vast amount of equipment, including countless artillery pieces. Among these, some stood out, partly because of their ballistic performance or because of the quantity.

The 76mm M1942 (ZiS-3), the 'divisional gun', had very good ballistic performance, so it could not only be used as a field gun, but also as an anti-tank weapon.

The German units recognized the potential of these guns, which were initially introduced unchanged as the 7.62cm FK 296(r) – the 'r' indicates *Russisch* (Russian) origin – and used ammunition captured from the Red Army. Since these stocks were limited, some of the captured guns were modified by boring out (enlarging) the cartridge chamber in the breech block so that German-manufactured ammunition (7.5cm PaK 40) could be fired. In this configuration, the gun was designated as 7.62cm PaK 36(r).

Both guns were assigned to the PzJg units as welcome reinforcements, which they used with much success. Since the first self-propelled PzJg had proved useful within their capabilities, it was obvious to use the 7.62cm PaK 36(r) to create a new type of self-propelled gun.

Again, mechanically outdated or obsolete tanks were used for this purpose. Initially, the effective captured weapon was mounted on the chassis of the *Flammpanzer* (flamethrower tank) variant of the PzKpfw II Ausf D. Although the Christie-type running gear allowed high speeds and acceptable cross-country mobility, the type was not a success.

At the same time, it was decided to use older PzKpfw 38(t). Although some armoured divisions were still equipped with the light tank throughout 1942, the type was seen as obsolescent.

With both solutions, the crew remained largely unprotected, both against enemy fire and the weather.

When the German 7.5cm PaK 40 became available in sufficient numbers, it was also be used to create further self-propelled guns. The weapon was mounted on the chassis of the PzKpfw II Ausf F and the PzKpfw 38(t) and fitted with improved armour protection.

The 7.5cm PaK 97/38 was far inferior to the 7.5cm PaK 40 in terms of ballistic performance. For anti-tank combat, the PaK 97/38 was limited to firing hollow charge ammunition, which had poor accuracy due to a low muzzle velocity. Maximum combat range of was some 1,000m.

	7.5cm PaK 40 (*)	7.62cm PaK 36(r) (**)

Ballistic Performance

	7.5cm PaK 40 (*)	7.62cm PaK 36(r) (**)
Shell size	7.5cm	7.62cm
Barrel length	3,450mm	3,895mm
Calibre	L/46	L/48.4
Muzzle velocity (metres per second – mps)	770mps (PzGr 39)	706mps (PzGr 39)

Penetration Data

Ammunition Range	7.5cm PzGr 39	7.62cm PzGr 39
100m	99mm	98mm
500m	91mm	90mm
1,000m	81mm	82mm
1,500m	72mm	73mm
2,000m	63mm	65mm

Ammunition Range	7.5cm PzGr 40	7.62cm PzGr 40
100m	126mm	135mm
500m	108mm	111mm
1,000m	87mm	94mm
1,500m	Ineffective	75mm
2,000m	Ineffective	58mm

Ammunition Range	7.5cm Gr 38 HL/C	7.62cm Gr 38 HL/C
100m	100mm	100mm
500m	100mm	100mm
1,000m	100mm	100mm
1,500m	100mm	100mm
2,000m	Ineffective	Ineffective

(*) This weapon had the same performance as the 7.5cm KwK 40, the 7.5cm StuK 40 and the 7.5cm PaK 39, as used in tanks, assault guns and tank hunter/destroyers.
(**) This weapon was produced by re-boring the chamber of captured Russian 76mm Divisional Gun Model 1936.

- PzSfl 1 (7.62cm PaK[r] auf Fgst PzKw II Ausf D), 150 built
- PzSfl 2 (7.62cm PaK[r] auf Fgst PzKw 38[t]t), 344 built
- PzJg II (7.5cm PaK 40/2 auf Fgst PzKw II Ausf F), 533 built
- PzJg 38(t) (7.5cm PaK 40/3 auf Fgst PzKw 38[t]), 275 built
- PzJg 38(t) (7.5cm PaK 40/3 auf Fgst Gw 38[t]), 942 built
  (Note: auf Fgst [*auf Fahrgestell* – on chassis])

The various self-propelled tank destroyers (7.5cm and 7.62cm) remained in production until early 1944 and were used on all battlefronts until the end of the war. The vehicles gave the tank destroyer units a high degree of mobility, and were also very effective in a defensive battle.

The development of even more powerful self-propelled tank destroyers was to continue, partly because of their undeniably good performance, partly out of sheer necessity. As the war progressed, the demand for tanks and assault guns exceeded the capacities of the German armaments industry, so improvisation was necessary where and whenever possible.

In 1941, German forces fighting on the Eastern Front became desparately short of anti-tank weapons. One simple solution was to re-purpose French-built tanks – here, the R-35 – that had been captured intact in 1940.

Russia: 1942–1943 **3**

Assault guns were an important milestone in the development of the tank destroyer. As late as 1941, the turretless vehicles were clearly identified as an effective means of offensive warfare. Combatting enemy tanks was secondary.

The *Richtlinien über den Einsatz der Sturmartillerie* (Basic Rules for Combat Use of Assault Artillery) doctrine, published in May 1940, stated:

> The assault gun is primarily an attack weapon. It can only fire in the direction of travel. To support an infantry attack, *Sturmartillerie* [StuArt – assault artillery] engages enemy heavy infantry weapons that cannot be destroyed quickly or effectively by the other weapons. In support of tanks (when attached to tank divisions) in the attack, it takes over part of the tasks of the PzKpfw IV and eliminates any enemy anti-tank guns appearing in front of the frontline.
>
> In case of enemy counterattacks with tanks, the tank destroyers intervene in the fight first. The assault artillery battalion fights enemy heavy weapons supporting their tank counterattack. Only when the tank destroyers are withdrawn does the assault artillery engage the enemy tanks. For this purpose, the assault guns drive towards the enemy to effective ranges, hold and then destroy them with tank shells.
>
> The use of an individual StuG battery as part of a division is the exception. Assault batteries deployed in this way must be cleared for their actual tasks at any time and must then be able to line up with full ammunition and equipment.

This doctrine came into being before the beginning of the French campaign. The restrictions described are understandable, and primarily concern the allocation of combat tasks.

According to this doctrine, the assault gun units were to be attached to other divisions normally in battalion size. The most concentrated and massed

Opposite: A well-camouflaged *Marder* (Marten) III Ausf H. The type utilized the service-proven chassis of the PzKpfw 38(t) and is armed with a 7.5cm PaK 40. The availability of this weapon initiated the design of further types to provide hard-pressed anti-tank units fighting in the east with heavier weapons and much-needed mobility.

By the end of 1941, the dire shortage of effective anti-tank weapons forced the use of captured Russian guns. Although the retreating Red Army left vast stocks of ammunition, German military planners decided to modify these guns to fire German ammunition. Those converted were designated as the 7.62cm PaK 36(r).

approach was seen as a prerequisite for a quick success that would enable the infantry, mountain or tank divisions to perform the breakthrough. However, the number of assault guns was never sufficient to allocate a StuGAbt to all divisions, except at clearly defined focal points. Here allocation would be a battery (six StuG, but often less due to combat losses), which deviated from the doctrine. In view of the far superior medium and heavy tanks that the Red Army was to throw into the fight shortly after the invasion, these considerations soon became invalid. The tank destroyers of the infantry and armoured divisions were not up to the challenge; neither 3.7cm nor 5cm PaK guns could successfully operate at the required combat ranges.

Those units that had attached assault gun units had to use them to fight the Russian tanks. In emergencies, the assault guns fought any target and the concerns of the senior officers in the assault artillery became irrelevant.

Countless reports from the infantry prove the (relative) effectiveness of the assault guns, despite their inferiority in terms of weaponry. At sometimes very close range, the T-34 and KV-1 were stopped, but only after a large amount of ammunition had been expended. Well-aimed shots at the few sensitive components damaged the running gear or jammed the turret.

The German attackers were helped by the low combat efficiency of the Russian tank crews. Although the soldierly toughness and bravery of the individual Russian soldier was fully recognized by the Germans, their training proved to be inadequate and the proportion of illiterates was high. The middle and lower leadership of the Red Army, NCOs and officers, were inferior to their German adversaries. Combat morale on the Russian side was also often poor.

On the German side, *Auftragstaktik* (mission tactics) were to prove their worth. The principle that every rank should be able to carry out the tasks of the next higher one resulted in tactically adept and well-motivated soldiers.

The inadequate radio equipment of the Russian units further hampered their fundamental technical superiority.

During the fighting for the Crimea in March 1942, strong Russian units were concentrated on the Kerch isthmus to relieve the hard-pressed, strategically important city of Sevastopol to the west. Here, in addition to the 22.PzDiv, StuGAbt 197 was also deployed, unusually for defence; in a determined counterattack, an assault gun became a tank destroyer. At this point, the division was only equipped with short-barrelled guns.

The battalion was deployed with two operational batteries at the beginning

In spring 1943, the self-propelled *Hornisse* (hornet), armed with an 8.8cm PaK 43/41, entered service and was probably the most effective of all German tank destroyers. Later, on orders from Adolf Hitler, the type was renamed *Nashorn* (rhinoceros). A total of around 500 vehicles had been completed by the end of the war.

In 1940, the first purpose-designed self-propelled tank destroyer, armed with a Czechoslovak-built 4.7cm PaK(t), was completed. The type entered service in 1941 and gradually replaced the PzJg 1, which in turn were issued to training units.

In general, road conditions on the *Ost* (East) Front were poor, particularly for wheeled vehicles. Also, the lack of tracked and half-track tractors forced German military planners to improvise. Here, an Opel *Maultier* (mule), a standard truck fitted with a half-track bogie, is in use as a tractor for towing a 7.5cm PaK 40.

of March 1942 with the XXXXII. Army Corps on the defensive front. It played a decisive role in the successful defence against the attacks by the Soviets on 13 to 16 March and 19 March, which were carried out with heavy use of medium, heavy and super-heavy tanks. The battalion succeeded in knocking out 70 tanks, and repelled numerous infantry attacks. This was the first time the division deployed the StuG battalion in defence against such massive tank attacks. Their experiences were as follows:

1.) Use of assault guns for anti-tank defence:
The assault guns, as a distinctly offensive weapon, should generally be held back in defence and only used for counterattacks when the enemy breaks into our *Hauptkampflinie* [HKL – main line of resistance]. It became apparent here that, with the current low operational strength of our own infantry and the considerable numerical superiority of tank, infantry and artillery deployment on the Soviet side, a counterattack with assault guns was not an option. Our assault guns were therefore deployed as the smallest unit, in platoons of three guns, directly in or in front of the HKL, in order to prevent any incursion by enemy tanks and, above all, by the following infantry.

2.) Preparation for the operation:

The selection of a concealed staging area and the expected direction of attack must be made in close consultation with our infantry. A knocked-out enemy tank gave one assault gun the best cover for days.

3.) Combat:

The platoon leader must absolutely bring his platoon – transmission of orders by radio – into the flank of the detected approaching enemy tank attack, without regard to his own open flanks. This way our probability of hitting the enemy, whose lateral target area is larger and more vulnerable than its front, is much greater. The element of surprise is crucial; we often carried out deceptive movements to lure the Red Army tanks out and take advantage of their miserable observation means. Using this tactic was made easier for us by the fact that the enemy tanks almost always attacked side-on or at an acute angle to the HKL, which also clarified target selection for individual guns in most cases. Independent fire was opened abruptly on the command of the platoon leader, usually at around 800m to 1,000m range in the case of an approaching mass attack. The firing must be rapid and accurate. The Russian T-34 crew usually got off only a single shot for every three to four rounds fired by our StuG, with considerably less accuracy (*). If assault guns

The StuG Ausf F8, armed with a 7.5cm StuK 40, became a very effective tank destroyer. This vehicle is in service with the anti-tank battalion of *Luftwaffen-Feld-Division* 14, which was stationed in Norway until the end of the war.

are fired upon by a T-34 and super-heavy Russian tanks, frequent and rapid changes of position under cover of smoke screen have proved effective. If possible, another gun immediately takes up the fight against the attacker.

Subsequently, during the heavy fighting of the last few days, despite the heaviest shelling, there was only one total loss. This assault gun could have been recovered but, only because our infantry had to retreat, it had to be blown up.

4.) Behaviour of our infantry:

A prerequisite for the success of a defensive fight by assault guns is that our infantry

The StuG Ausf G was the most produced variant, with some 8,500 built. Interestingly, a significant proportion was not assigned to assault artillery units, but to *Panzerjäger-Kompanien* (PzJgKp – tank destroyer companies) in infantry divisions.

remained in the HKL under all circumstances, even if some Soviet tanks had entered the line. Enemy infantry went along with their tanks only at the beginning of an attack. In the process they suffered heavy casualties, many due to fire from our assault guns ricocheting off their target. Later, attacks were made by a lone tank. However, if our infantry fell back, the Russians immediately advanced and occupied our positions in the HKL. Under these circumstances, a counterattack was usually not unsuccessful, and always costly.

5.) Firing procedure and choice of ammunition:

A StuG Ausf G in service with an unidentified *Luftwaffe-Feld-Division* (LwFeldDiv – air force field division).

During any mass attacks, fire had to be opened at a minimum range of 600m, but a considerable number of the kills were achieved at longer range. When the Soviet tanks stopped at a range of 1,000m to 1,200m and opened fire, it was quite impossible for our assault guns to approach any closer in the completely open, uncovered terrain. Moreover, the assault guns could not advance beyond the HKL because of mines laid by our troops or a barrage of our own artillery.

When fighting the T-26 and BT, total destruction was achieved at any range using impact fuses, sometimes fired with delay.

High-explosive shells with impact fuses were fired against T-34 tanks, sometimes with delay. Then, at a range of some 600m, the effective firing was carried out with 7.5cm Gr 38 (HL) (**).

Effect: Complete destruction of the entire running gear, total destruction of the interior, killing of the entire crew (***). In most cases, the tanks burnt out.

A Red Army KV-1, which fired at another assault gun from a range of 1,200m, could be not destroyed and was only damaged.

Ammunition consumption was naturally quite high; in addition to the tanks, enemy infantry,

anti-tank guns and field artillery also had to be engaged. Therefore, in addition to those 100 rounds (****) stored in each gun, sufficient quantities of ammunition were stacked in our staging areas. After each defeated attack, ammunition was replenished. The last operational armoured ammunition carrier (*****) was constantly on the move to replenish stocks.

6.) Summary:

Even a massed enemy tank attack can be beaten off in most cases by an assault gun platoon with three guns, but only if it is properly led, kept mobile and has sufficient ammunition. The platoon leader and his crews the must be tactically alert. Then, even in the face of a numerically superior force of Red Army tanks, they will not be ruffled, and if they remain confident, success is assured.

The PzSfl 2, later called the *Marder* III, was an effective weapon due to it being armed with a 7.62cm PaK 36(r). Offensive use of these lightly armoured vehicles was not advisable and and many fell victim to Red Army long-range weapons.

The superstructure of the PzSfl 2 was fabricated from riveted 10mm and 14.5mm armour plates, thus the crew was only provisionally protected against light infantry weapons. The considerable height of the vehicle was thought of as a disadvantage.

(*) Other German reports state the hit results on Russian tanks as ranging from good to very good.

(**) From spring 1942 onwards, the 7.5cm Gr 38 HL/A and HL/B hollow-charge shells became available, and this allowed a penetration of 60mm to 75mm armour at any realistic range.

(***) The hits described were from shaped charges that probably penetrated the thinner hull sides and detonated the fuel tanks. As a result, the vehicle was completely destroyed. The previous bracketing fire was necessary due to the low velocity of the Gr 38 HL and the resulting poor accuracy.

(****) In fact, the StuG units removed the factory-mounted ammunition holders, which held 44 rounds. Often, larger quantities were carried.

(*****) SdKfz 252 *leichter gepanzerter Munitionstransportwagen* (le gep MunTrsptWg – light armoured ammunition carrier).

Langrohr

With the introduction of the 7.5cm StuK 40 in the first half of 1942, the importance of the assault guns increased noticeably. The units that were still in action on the Eastern Front received the powerful vehicles from front-line depots which often resulted in mixed equipment. In one case, a complete complement of 21 *Langrohr-Geschützen* (long-barrelled guns) was delivered, but instead of the original equipment being returned it was kept hidden due to the on-going desperate supply situation.

Newly established assault gun detachments, or those units that had been re-equipped, either on the frontline or at their home garrison, were issued with the standard allotment of 21 new production assault guns (7.5cm [*lang*]).

Three years later, the doctrine was to be adapted to the realities at the front:

Tasks

Armoured self-propelled guns are an assault weapon and provide immediate combat support to the infantry through mobility and firepower. In attack, they assault enemy front-line positions and reserve concentrations, especially his heavy weapons. In defence, they support counterattacks because they are the most effective anti-tank defence.

In 1942, and even more so in 1943, Russia proved able to increase tank

From 1943, many PzJgAbt were being issued with assault guns in place of the poorly armoured self-propelled types. Here, the commander of a StuG III Ausf G, armed with a 7.5cm *Sturmhaubitz* (StuH – assault howitzer), has positioned his vehicle in bushes, ready to ambush enemy armour.

Despite the obvious superiority of purpose-designed assault guns and self-propelled tank destroyers, experimental types continued to be developed until the end of the war. One of those was this semi-armoured SdKfz 11 which has been modified to mount a 7.5cm PaK 42 L/70, as used in the PzKpfw V Panther.

production to an unheard-of extent. The Allied aid supplies were a vital support for survival. German industry could not keep up with the sheer number of tanks required, since there was a lack of production capacity and dearth of raw materials.

During this period, the losses in the Panzer divisions could hardly be compensated; assault guns had to fill these gaps. For some units, the turretless vehicles were to be used instead of tanks in new formations and replenishments.

Panzer Division 43

Simplified, the new organizational standard of PzDiv 43 was to have two tank battalions. It was planned to equip one with the new PzKpfw V Panther, the other with PzKpfw IV. The divisional tank destroyer section had three companies each with 14 self-propelled 7.5cm PaK. In addition, there were various support units.

PzGrenDiv 43

The new *Panzergrenadier* (PzGren – armoured infantry) Division 43 was to have, in addition to two PzGrenRgt, a PzAbt (StuG) with 45 StuG. The PzJgAbt had two companies of 7.5cm PaK self-propelled guns, one company of towed 7.5cm PaK and one SturmFlak company issued with 12 SdKfz 10/4 mounting a 2cm FlaK 30.

Weapons – Technical Data

	7.5cm StuK 40	8.8cm PaK 43/2
Mounted	StuG III and StuG IV	*Ferdinand*
Mounted (modified)	le PzJg IV	*Jagdpanther*
	le PzJg 38 *Hetzer*	
Shell size	7.5cm	8.8cm
Barrel length	3,855mm	6,300mm
Calibre length	L/48	L/71
Rate of fire (rpm)	Ten	Ten
Barrel life span	4,000 rounds	3,000 rounds

Ammunition

	7.5cm SprGr 34	8.8cm SprGr 43
High explosive		
Muzzle velocity	550mps	750mps
Range (maximum)	8,100m	1,4200m

	7.5cm PzGr 39	8.8cm PzGr 39/1
Armour piercing		
Muzzle velocity	750mps	1,000mps
Penetration 100m	99mm	170mm
Penetration 500m	91mm	155mm
Penetration 1,000m	81mm	138mm
Penetration 1,500m	2mm	122mm
Penetration 2,000m	63mm	110mm

	7.5cm PzGr 40	8.8cm PzGr 40/43
Armour piercing		
Muzzle velocity	920mps	1,140mps
Penetration 100m	126mm	202mm
Penetration 500m	108mm	185mm
Penetration 1,000m	87mm	165mm
Penetration 1,500m	69mm	147mm
Penetration 2,000m	–	132mm

	7.5cm Gr 38 HL/C	8.8cm Gr 39 HL
Muzzle velocity	450mps	600mps
Penetration 100m	90-100mm	90mm
Penetration 500m	90-100mm	90mm
Penetration 1,000m	90-100mm	90mm
Penetration 1,500m	–	90mm
Penetration 2,000m	–	–

The fact that the tank destroyer units should now have been completely or almost completely equipped with armoured self-propelled guns testifies to the inadequacy of the towed PaK on the Russian Front. But this goal was never achieved.

Some 'elite' formations, the InfDiv Großdeutschland, as well as SS-Division Leibstandarte Adolf Hitler, SS-Division Das Reich and SS-Division Totenkopf, each received a StuGAbt.

At almost the same time as the 7.5cm PaK 40 began to be issued to front-line units, large numbers of 76.2mm M1942 (ZiS-3) anti-tank guns, captured from the Red Army and re-chambered to fire German ammunition, became available. The weapon was designated 7.62cm PaK 36(r) and mounted on the earliest versions of the *Marder* III.

Sturmgeschütz – Technical Data		
	Sturmgeschütz Ausf G	Panzerjäger Tiger (P) Ferdinand
Chassis	PzKpfw III	VK 4501(P)
Weight	23,900kg	65,000kg
Engine	Maybach HL 120TRM	Two Maybach HL 120TRM
Speed (maximum)	40kph	30kph
Range (road)	195km	150km
Range (cross country)	95km	90km
Main weapon	7.5cm StuK 40	8.8cm PaK 43/2
Secondary weapons	One MG 34 Two MP 40	One MG 34 Two MP 40
Armour (front)	80mm	200mm
Armour (side)	30mm	80mm

By the end of 1942, the first tank destroyer divisions of the newly established *Luftwaffe* field divisions were also to receive 10 *Langrohr-Geschützen* each. Unlike the artillery assault gun battalion, *Sturmhaubitzen* (StuH – assault howitzers) were normally not assigned.

Over the year 1942, the number of combat-ready long-barrelled assault guns increased continuously, but the exact numbers are not known. It was not until the reinstatement of Guderian to an active role, in March 1943, that a consolidated inventory listing was to be introduced. On 14 April 1943, a total of 415 assault guns were reported as being operational on all battlefronts (excluding the reserve army). A further 146 were in repair and 205 were being stored in supply depots. The vast majority of these vehicles at that time were armed with the 7.5cm StuK L/43 or StuK L/48.

A total of 47 assault guns with 7.5cm KwK L/24 *Kurzrohr* (*kurz* – short barrel) were still available, but all were with units of *Heeresgruppe Nord* (Army Group North) and *Heeresgruppe Mitte* (Army Group Centre). Only 14 assault howitzers (10.5cm StuH) were in the inventory of two divisions of the assault artillery.

Units that were not under the command of the artillery were deployed according to deviating operational principles. These obviously extended to the necessary fight against the Soviet tanks that were arriving in ever greater numbers. The StuG units finally became PzJg.

In January 1943, the commander of 9.Army reported to his superiors at *Heeresgruppe Mitte:*

> Experiences during the large-scale Russian attack against the main elements of 9.Army during the period 25 November to 16 December 1942.
>
> *Sturmgeschütz:* The *lang* and *kurz* are the best anti-tank defence. The low firing height makes it easier to move into firing positions. The StuG *lang* has an armour-piercing effect up to a range of 1,200m. It can be used to successfully engage enemy tanks that are sensitive to fire from light and medium anti-tank guns. For StuG *kurz*, the 7.5cm hollow charge (Gr 38 [H]) shell must currently be used for anti-tank fire. The effect is sufficient, even if it does not reach that of the 7.5cm PzGr 39.
> An assault gun battery with six StuG can effectively stop a Russian tank brigade (*).

(*) In 1943, a typical Red Army T-34-equipped tank brigade was issued with approximately 65 tanks.

This overwhelmingly positive assessment proved several certainties that were to shape the year 1943. The combat effectiveness of German tank and assault gun units was now clearly superior to that of the Red Army. By making the best possible use of the available equipment, sometimes overwhelming successes could be achieved.

Nevertheless, the period of *Blitzkrieg* was to draw to a close at the end of 1942 with the unsuccessful siege of Stalingrad and defeat looming in North Africa. In the summer of 1943, the German army command attempted a last large-scale operation in the area around Belgorod and Kursk. On the occasion of this offensive, new weapons were to be used for the first time.

Ferdinand – StuG or PzJg?

During the pre-production phase of the PzKpfw VI Ausf E Tiger heavy tank, two developments competed with each other, the *Versuchskraftwagen* (VK – experimental motor vehicle) 4501(H) from the Henschel company and the VK 4501(P) from the design bureau of Dr Ferdinand Porsche.

An unusual petrol-electric drive system was chosen for the 'Porsche-*Kampfwagen*': two Porsche air-cooled engines drove Siemens-Schukert generators, which produced power for Siemens 230kw electric motors that were directly connected to the rear-mounted drive sprockets. The running gear consisted of six wheels fitted in pairs on three bogies, which were mounted on lateral torsion bars.

In July 1942, the tanks were subjected to thorough testing at the Kummersdorf proving ground. The results were clear: the performance and operational safety of the mechanically more conservative vehicle from Henschel were markedly better, and so the vehicle was to go into series production as the PzKpfw VI

A Red Army propaganda photograph. Both the 14.5mm PTRS and 14.5mm PTRD, heavy anti-tank rifles, were capable of penetrating the 30mm side armour of many German tanks and assault guns, but only at close range. (Getty)

Ausf E Tiger. Albert Speer, *Reichsministerium für Bewaffnung und Munition* (Minister of Armaments and Munitions), demanded a halt to production of the VK 4501(P), despite Hitler having stated his preference for the type. However, Porsche had anticipated this and had already initiated the production of 100 hulls. These were now stored at Nibelungenwerk in St Valentin, Austria, the facility where the prototypes were built.

In order to make the best possible use of these hulls, it was decided to utilize them to develop a heavy assault gun. Hitler personally demanded the installation of the new 8.8cm PaK L/71, so that it would be quickly available under the heaviest armour protection at the front. The new specifications, drawn up in September 1942, provided for much heavier armour than on the basic vehicle. While the front armour of the VK 4501(P) was already an impressive 100mm, the superstructure, which was completely redesigned for this project, now had 200mm of armour at the front. The thickness of the plates at the sides, rear of the hull and superstructure was 80mm – an extraordinarily high level of protection.

The main weapon was the 8.8cm PaK 43/2 L/71, the most powerful anti-tank weapon available at the time. Thanks to the large calibre length, enormous rates of penetration could be achieved. Since the weapon had to be mounted in a rear-positioned casemate-type superstructure, the existing hulls and suspension had to be extensively modified. This work was carried out by Eisenwerke Oberdonau between January and April 1943.

In 1942, the US began supplying military equipment to the Soviet Union under the Lend-Lease Program. Here, a Red Army officer inspects his anti-tank troop that has been issued with the Willys MB Jeep to tow a Soviet-produced 45mm Model 1942 (M-42) semi-automatic gun. (Getty)

The PzSfl 1 was of simple construction. The captured Russian weapon was built on a simple bridge, mounted transversely on the hull of the tank. The operation had no effective protection against enemy fire and the weather. Some 150 were built.

The two engines and the power generators, including the cooling system, were moved to the front. The electric drive remained in the rear of the hull. The originally planned Porsche-type petrol engines could not be used since, in order to provide the required electrical power, the engines had to be run at full throttle during operation, which led to permanent overheating. This problem could never be solved by the Porsche team and so it was decided to install two Maybach HL 120 engines – the same type as fitted in the PzKpfw III and PzKpfw IV – between the driver and the fighting compartment. The cramped conditions led to a number of problems; the supply of combustion air to the engines was unsatisfactory, and the cooling of the two engines and the generators was also inadequate.

In April 1943, the production of 90 heavy assault guns was in full swing at Nibelungenwerk. Hitler had personally intervened, insisting that these vehicles take part in the planned offensive at Kursk.

Initially, the vehicles had been promised to the assault artillery; the high armour and effective armament seemed to suit the offensive approach of this type of weapon. In fact, for a while, consideration was was given to producing a version fitted with a 21cm mortar.

Now the *Generalinspekteur der Panzertruppe* (GenInsp d PzTrp – Inspector General of Armoured Forces) was to intervene. Guderian insisted that these vehicles were assigned to the *schnellen Truppen* (rapid forces), or the *Panzertruppe*, as it was called from 1943. The designation was changed to *Panzerjäger* Tiger (P) and classified as the SdKfz 184, and became generally known as the *Ferdinand* – but was later renamed *Elefant*.

On 30 May 1943, *Waffen-Merkblatt* (weapons leaflet) No.11 was published, and noted of the *Ferdinand*:

> Due to its armament and heavy armour, this is a particularly powerful weapon to fight tanks and support attacks against strong enemy resistance and also permanent fighting installations (fortified positions and bunkers). But its high weight and limited cross-country mobility restricts the possibilities of use and require particularly detailed terrain reconnaissance prior to deployment.

Consequently, these vehicles, which were more or less born out of the embarrassment of making the best use of existing materiel, were to be used both as assault guns and tank destroyers.

Shortly before the offensive began, two battalions, *schwere Panzerjäger Abteilung* (s PzJgAbt – heavy tank destroyer battalion) 653 and s PzJgAbt 654, each with 45 vehicles, were ready for combat. Together with the *Sturmpanzer-Abteilung* (StuPzAbt – assault tank battalion) 216, the units were attached to s PzJgRgt 656, whose staff coordinated the operations.

This first mission did not go well. From a field report:

> The s PzJgRgt 656, deployed as part of 9.Army, was joined by the 86.InfDiv for the attack. To create lanes through the suspected minefields, two PzKp (Fkl)(*) were attached to the regiment. The very heavy enemy artillery bombardment (on the first day 100 heavy and 172 light guns, 386 rocket launchers and an unknown number of mortars) crushed our infantry attack.
>
> Due to this fact, the *Ferdinand* and assault tanks could not carry the attack fast enough into the depths of the defender, but stood in the terrain for a long time. This attracted the concentrated enemy artillery fire. Enemy anti-tank close-combat were also active. Here, the lack of machine-gun armament took its toll and resulted in high casualties.
>
> Total losses: 19 *Ferdinand*, the majority destroyed by a direct artillery hit on the engine covers. Four were stopped by a short-circuit in the electrical system and subsequently caught fire. Ten assault tanks were blown up by the crews after mine or artillery hits.
>
> Temporary losses due to mines: 40 *Ferdinand*, of which 20 had been repaired by 11 July, and 17 StuPz, of which nine had been repaired by the same date.
>
> For the most part, only a few track links were damaged, and in some cases running wheels and swing arms. The high loss due to mine damage occurred despite the deployment of two PzKp [Fkl](*). These vehicles were not effective in the heavy artillery fire.

A well-camouflaged Nashorn tank destroyer positioned at the entrance to a collection point for vehicles in service with an anti-tank battalion attached to PzGrenDiv Großdeutschland. Note the helmet symbol used to identify the division. (Getty)

Some of the radio-guided demolition carriers and some control vehicles were already put out of action in the staging areas.

Each company cleared up two lanes through the minefield. Because of the heavy artillery fire, the sappers failed to mark the cleared lanes, which were therefore not obvious to the *Ferdinand* crews.

Despite the high losses, the *Ferdinand* and StuG always achieved their ordered objectives. In a bold advance, the StuPzAbt broke through the Russians' third position, some 5km ahead of its infantry element. This success had to be abandoned as no tank reserves were brought up from the rear and the infantry lacked the strength to follow. This fact clearly shows that the decisive success against an enemy in a deeply staggered position system and strong artillery superiority cannot be achieved in conjunction with the infantry. If s PzJgRgt 656 had been coupled with a tank division and the tank attack had been deeply structured with tanks and riflemen on armoured half-tracks in several waves, the successes would have been exploited quickly and the breakthrough would undoubtedly have been achieved with fewer losses.

Weapons: The 8.8cm PaK 43/2 has proven its worth, but the lack of an MG proved to

German anti-tank guns from 1935 to 1943: Although the 8.8cm PaK 43/41 had exceptional ballistic performance, it weighed 4,300kg and was almost 1.9m high, both of which made it cumbersome to move and very difficult to camouflage.

be a disadvantage. Therefore, 12 PzKpfw III were attached to the *Ferdinand* for close protection and to engage soft targets.

Armour protection: The front armour has not been penetrated in any case, but the side armour has been holed in some cases by 7.62cm at close range. The engine cover and the roof of the fighting compartment have been penetrated by artillery direct hits.

(*) These *Panzer-Kompanie* (*Funklenk*) (PzKp [Fkl] – tank company [radio control]) were issued with the Borgward B IV *Sprengladungsträger* (demolition charge carrier).

During the fighting in the Kursk salient, these 70,000kg vehicles were used in the manner of assault guns to attack well-prepared emplacements. The terrain, churned up by artillery fire, made it almost impossible to advance. In this situation, the extremely effective tank destroyer gun could not be used to its full potential. In summary, this first mission shows the immense difficulties associated with the use of such heavy combat vehicles.

The remaining vehicles were to be used with great success by s PzJgAbt 653 as mobile interception weapons in the autumn 1943 battles around Nikopol.

On 16 December 1943, the remnants of s PzJgAbt 653 and s PzJgAbt 654 were transferred to Austria for general overhaul and replenishment. The remaining *Ferdinand*, now called *Elefant*, were merged into s PzJgAbt 653.

Later missions by the battalion in Russia were similarly successful, but only defensively. The 1./s PzAbt 653 was sent to Italy with 11 *Elefant* to fight the Allied forces that had landed near Anzio. Due to the extremely difficult, mountainous terrain, the mission was less than satisfactory.

The assault gun gradually became the weapon of the tank destroyer troops.

The First *Jagdpanzer* 4

In March 1943, assault guns were supplied for the first time in larger numbers to branches of the armed forces other than the assault artillery. Initially, the three Panzer divisions that were destroyed at Stalingrad (14.PzDiv, 16.PzDiv and 24.PzDiv) each received a *Panzer-Sturmgeschütz-Abteilung* (PzStuGAbt – armoured assault gun battalion). This was followed in June by the PzGrenDiv (created from infantry division [mot]), which were in the process of being formed.

But Hitler had already issued a *Führer-Entscheidung* (decision) in March:

> The assault guns remain with the artillery as before and continue to have the purpose of serving the infantry as armoured escort artillery. Whenever assault guns are handed over to a PzDiv, they will during this time come under the care of the GenInsp d PzTrp.

These lines seem to imply only a temporary transfer of the assault guns. However, this question cannot be answered conclusively. Basically, this decision was driven by the German Reich losing the ability to conduct operational warfare after the aborted Kursk offensive. The consolidation of defensive structures now had to be given more attention.

Since the assault guns on the Eastern Front had proven to be extremely successful in the fight against the numerically superior Russian tanks, it was decided towards the end of 1943 to assign one company of these vehicles to each of the tank destroyer sections in infantry and mountain divisions. This meant that they were also subordinate to the *Panzertruppe*. Although this undoubtedly strengthened the combat power of the tank destroyer units, the small number of vehicles (10 to 14) meant that offensive deployment was virtually impossible.

Opposite: A column of German military vehicles moves through a village under the supervision of US soldiers. The Panzer IV/70 (V) is from the last production batch, which were not fitted with *Panzerschürzen* (armour side skirts) due to the desperate shortage of armoured steel and the loss of manufacturing facilities caused by the Allied round-the-clock bombing campaign.

The Messerschmitt Me 323 *Gigant* (giant) gave the German military an effective means of strategic air transport. The six-engine aircraft had a normal payload of 11,000kg, which allowed it to carry a *Marder* III.

Consequently, assault guns became tank destroyers – *Jagdpanzer* (JgdPz – hunter tank) – and the intended establishment of the assault artillery moved into the distant future.

This measure was not without controversy at the time. Despite the increase in production (792 StuG were manufactured in 1942, increasing to more than 3,000 in 1943), not all expectations could be met. Beginning in 1940, the artillery had insisted on the originally planned allocation of one StuGAbt in each infantry division. The fulfilment of these ambitious planning goals was, however, not possible because of the lack of manufacturing capacity.

The *General der Artillerie* Fritz Lindemann complained in a letter to the chief of the general staff, *Generaloberst* Kurt Zeitzler:

The StuArt is indeed the backbone of our infantry, which is often confronted with the most difficult tasks. StuG achieve the highest scores of all armoured vehicles and they have, so far, knocked out more than 12,000 enemy tanks. Assault guns have the lowest own casualties and have the highest percentage of operational vehicles.

The increase in assault gun production has already been ordered by Führer decree. Contrary to the prescribed concentrated deployment of assault guns in StuGAbt, distribution of the weapon remains fragmented. On 1 December 1943 there were:

- StuArt units: 54 percent
- Panzer units: 25.3 percent
- PzJg units of InfDiv: 5.5 percent
- PzJg units of *Luftwaffe* Field Divisions: 2.2 percent
- Waffen-SS units: 13 percent

Based on the conviction that the assault artillery will continue to gain importance in the coming year for the fight against the growing Russian assault artillery and tanks, I propose a clear delineation of development and responsibility:

The crews of assault guns tried various ways of improving the armour on their vehicles. Here, the surfaces on both sides of the gun have been filled with concrete. Note the crew has the decorated *Saukopfblende* (pig´s head) mantlet.

The 7.5cm PaK 40 L/46 auf *Geschützwagen* (Gw – gun carrier) II utilized the chassis of the PzKpfw II Ausf D or Ausf E and was known as *Marder* II. The type was quickly designed to satisfy an urgent demand from units on the Eastern Front for a mobile anti-tank gun.

Panzer and PzGrenDiv shall receive conventional tanks for independent tactical and operational deployment.

StuG of all calibres should be provided in battalion size at army troop level for immediate support of infantry divisions.

These quite understandable demands could not be met; there was a lack not only of the necessary production capacity, but probably also of political will. Understandably, the priority of the *Organisationsabteilung* (OrgAbt – organization department) was to secure replacements for front-line losses, as well as supplies for new deployments, and here the utilization of all available production capacity was crucial.

Sturmgeschütz IV

Instead, the production ratio now shifted. In 1943, some 3,011 more assault guns were produced than PzKpfw IV. This development received a dampener on 23–26 November 1943, when the company Altmärkische Kettenwerk (Alkett) became the target of a devastating attack by Allied bombers, causing production output to decline sharply.

To compensate for the loss of production, it was now hastily decided to mount an assault gun superstructure on the hull of the PzKpfw IV: In fact, this had already been discussed at the beginning of the year. At that time, Krupp supplied plans for an improved PzKpfw IV with sloped armour and better running gear with wider tracks. The complete conversion of both the PzKpfw IV and the assault gun production to this new design was considered, but the project soon had to be abandoned for various reasons.

The assembly of the Kasemitt superstructure on an unchanged PzKpfw IV hull did not prove to be difficult. Minor problems arose only in the area of the driver's seat which, due to the longer hull, was positioned further forward in front of the superstructure. Consequently, an armoured box was fabricated to protect the driver.

The designation StuG IV was chosen, while the vehicles based on the ZW chassis were designated StuG III. A first series of 30 StuG IV were built by Daimler-Benz at their facilities in Berlin-Marienfeld. Then, Krupp-Gruson in Magdeburg-Buckau, the company that manufactured the PzKpfw IV, took over production and delivered 1,141 StuG IV by April 1945.

In the last quarter of 1942, the newly established *Luftwaffe Felddivisionen* (air force field divisions) began to be issued with self-propelled guns, including the 7.5cm PaK 40/2 *Marder* II. Note the crew has been issued with paratrooper-type helmets. (Getty)

Above: The wooden mock-up of the *Jagdpanzer* IV was built using an unmodified PzKpfw IV Ausf F chassis, identifiable by the armoured *Nebelkerzen-Abwurfvorrichtung* (NKAV – smoke grenade launcher) mounted on the rear plate.

Left: The corners of the front plate on the superstructure were rounded on the wooden mock-up – unusual on a German-designed vehicle. The same feature was used on the 0-series, but was omitted on later production *Jagdpanzer*. The correct cast *Saukopfblende* gun mantlet has yet to be fitted.

Above: The 60mm front armour on the *Jagdpanzer* IV prototype was impervious to fire from most Allied 75mm anti-tank weapons. When series production began, it would soon be increased to 80mm, but this caused the vehicle to become front-heavy.

7.5cm L/48 – The *Panzerjäger* Gun

The 7.5cm StuK 40, which entered service in 1942, was still an effective weapon against most enemy tanks in 1944. The most important type of ammunition was the 7.5cm PzGr 39. This projectile with an armour-piercing cap and a ballistic cover had an explosive charge that was triggered after penetrating the armour. The ballistic performance of this ammunition naturally decreased gradually as target range increased; at 1,000m, it still penetrated some 82mm of Soviet armour. This was sufficient for the T-34 and the KV, but the heavy *Josef Stalin* (JS) II was difficult to defeat in head-on combat.

On 26 June 1944, the office of the Genlinsp d PzTrp stated:

The PzGr 39 is sufficient to fight all British, US and Russian tank types, that have

The specialist towing gear indicates that this is a collection point for damaged German tank destroyers. The parked vehicles include two StuG III, two Panzer IV/70 (A) and a *Marder* III.

so far appeared, at combat ranges of 600m to 1,200m. Even the newly introduced JS-II, with over 100mm thick armour, can be fought successfully since the cast steel used is of a lower density.

The 7.5cm PzGr 40, a hard-core (tungsten) projectile, was also available. With a relatively small diameter and an aluminium alloy coating, this projectile had a lower mass than the conventional tank shell and achieved a higher velocity. The kinetic energy on impact was correspondingly much higher. However, since the penetration performance decreased disproportionately with increasing range, the ammunition was only used to combat heavily

Although the StuG IV had 80mm front armour, the driver's position has been reinforced with a sloping steel plate. Note the surface to the left of the gun has been filled with concrete.

armoured battle tanks at close ranges. Also, since tungsten was a scarce material, only comparatively small quantities of the valuable ammunition were available, and gunners were urged to use it only in an exceptional situation.

A hollow charge projectile, the 7.5cm Gr 38 HL/C, could also be fired in certain situations. On impact, the conical shell projected a high-temperature jet of armour-piercing particles.

Ballistic performance remained constant at all achievable ranges and, despite only having a small diameter, the effect on a crew was usually fatal. The HL/C shell used in 1944 could effectively pierce armour up to 100mm

Arys (Orzysz), Poland, on 20 October 1943: Adolf Hitler attends one of the regular meetings arranged for him to examine new projects and see the latest vehicles demonstrated. Here, he inspects an 0-series JgdPz IV which is parked next to a StuG III Ausf G armed with a 7.5cm StuK 40 L/43.

thick. However, due to the low velocity and the associated curved trajectory, accuracy was significantly lower. For this reason, multiple shots (bracketing) had to be used in action, with the associated high consumption of ammunition. The effective range was 1,000m to 1,500m.

The StuG IV was built on the hull of the PzKpfw IV Ausf H and Ausf J. The bow plate was 80mm thick, as was the front of the angular casemate superstructure. Theoretically, this should have made the vehicle safe against fire from 7.5cm weapons at ranges of over 1,000m, although this seems doubtful in practice, since the enemy also had effective anti-tank ammunition at their disposal in 1944.

The hull and superstructure sides were 30mm thick, but the rear plate was only 20mm. But again, the StuG IV, like the PzKpfw IV, was extremely vulnerable to lateral fire. The deployment of the vehicles had to be adapted according to these weaknesses, but this was not always achievable.

A major problem was the fact that Red Army used 14.5mm heavy anti-tank rifles (PTRS and PTRD) in huge quantities. These could penetrate the side armour of the assault gun when operated by brave men at close range, resulting in damage and serious injury to the crew members. For this reason, 5mm steel plates were attached to side rails on all German tanks and assault guns. The *Panzerschürzen* (armour skirts) proved effective against these close-range weapons, but were easily lost in action.

Combat

The 90.PzGrenDiv was one of the few large units to receive StuG IV. In the course of re-equipment in northern Italy, a total of 42 vehicles were delivered in February (the actual target was 45 vehicles). Apart from a number of unit strength reports, only a few combat-related files have survived. While the unit reported 38 combat-ready assault guns on 1 March, this number fell steadily

A *Maschinengewehr* (MG – machine gun) 42 was carried inside a tank destroyer as a self-defence weapon. Here, the crew has fabricated a mounting so that the weapon can be used to fire at Allied ground-attack aircraft.

The crew of this StuG IV has dug-in their vehicle behind cover on a hill that dominates the terrain. Despite the introduction of the more advanced tank destroyers, both the StuG III Ausf G and StuG IV remained in production until the war ended in 1945.

over the coming months to 29 on 1 April and only 13 on 1 June. By 1 July, not a single StuG IV was operational. The commander lamented the poor condition of his unit in his assessment:

> The loss of personnel, especially of leaders and specialists, is palpable. Due to the loss of vehicles, the stock of operational vehicles in the division has fallen to just 23 percent of the target and is therefore only mobile to a limited extent. Due to the unfavourable, difficult terrain of northern Italy, the *Wespe* battalion (*) is completely out of action. For the same reason, the StuG IV is no longer operational.

(*) *Wespe* (wasp) 10.5cm *Panzerhaubitze* (armoured howitzer).

Although no details were given, the high number of failures of the remaining vehicles undoubtedly resulted from the delicate final drives, which were overstressed on the steep slopes and tight curves of the Apennines and failed in large numbers. By the end of the year, after another re-equipment period, the number of serviceable assault guns rose again to 60–70 percent of the establishment strength.

When the assault guns were deployed correctly, they proved to be effective. On 26 April 1944, the commander of Fallschirmjäger-Regiment 3, *Oberst* Ludwig Heilmann, reported on the use of a single StuG IV of the 90.PzGrenDiv:

If assault guns are operated properly, they are an excellent weapon. A single assault gun kept the numerous enemy tanks at bay and at a distance for days at Monte Cassino.

But Hellman also stated:

The German tanks are obviously not suitable for use in the Italian theatre of war. They can hardly leave solid roads and can really only be used as mobile artillery. If a tank is needed, it is usually not combat-ready. One can get the impression that our tank crews no longer trust their weapons and feel inferior to the enemy tanks.

While units like the 90.PzGrenDiv were assigned a complete detachment of 45 StuG IV, the infantry divisions received only one company each for their PzJg detachment. On 23 June 1944, the commander of 12.InfDiv reported receiving ten StuG IV for its StuGAbt 1012, but noted succinctly:

StuGAbt 1012 has 60 percent combat-experienced soldiers and 40 percent young replacements. The unit has absolutely no experience in the use of assault guns.

In 1944, the typical infantry division on the Eastern Front was, in practice, engaged in fierce defensive battles against an overpowering opponent, the German army having lost the ability to conduct offensive operations in 1943. If one sets the combat front of a division at approximately 7–10km wide,

A 7.5cm PaK 42 L/70-armed Panzer IV/70 (V) parked on a cobbled street of a small town in the west of the Reich. The vehicle mounts a 7.5cm PaK 42 L/70 gun and has 80mm front armour, both of which began to be introduced from May 1944. This increased the front loading, necessitating the introduction of all-steel running wheels.

German maintenance engineers often had to work under very difficult conditions to keep vehicles in working order. Here, a team work to replace a running wheel bogie. Note the wheels are of the earlier, rubber-tyred type.

the inadequacy of its equipment becomes clear. If enemy armoured forces attacked, the few assault guns available had to advance to the breakthrough point. These long marches put a great strain on the equipment. In action, the StuG IV crew had to aim their vehicle at the targets, resulting in constant steering adjustments.

The GenInsp d PzTrp, Heinz Guderian, rejected the use of assault guns within the framework of his proposed *schnelle Truppen* (rapid forces) or *Panzertruppe*. In a note sent to a *Führer-Vortrag* (lecture to Hitler) on 26 June 1944, he made his view clear:

> The PzKpfw IV is currently our most mature tank design, in which every tank soldier has full confidence. The StuG on the same chassis, on the other hand, must be regarded as a makeshift solution that is considerably inferior to the StuG based on the PzKpfw III chassis. The final drives are the weak point of the chassis of the PzKpfw IV. Since the assault gun has to aim with the complete vehicle, the brakes – as well as the final drives – are constantly subjected to higher stress loads. These components therefore break with increasing regularity. At the same time, there seems to be a considerable bottleneck in the supply of spares.

In May 1944, PzJgAbt 389 of the 389.InfDiv was reorganized. In addition

to the staff company, the battalion still had its second company with 7.5cm PaK 40 (towed by *Raupenschlepper Ost* [RSO – fully tracked tractor east]) as well as the 3.Kp (FlaK) with 2cm FlaK 38. PzJgAbt 389 received, for the first time, StuG IV in company strength (10 or 14 vehicles according to *Kriegstärkenachweisungen* [KStN – standardized organizational structures] KStN 1149). This sub-unit was confusingly given the designation StuGAbt 1389 because, in 1944, all StuG units assigned to the divisions as sub-units with 10 or 14 vehicles were listed as battalions, despite being only at company strength. It was customary to give this unit the number of the infantry division, and to prefix it with the numeral '1'.

During the months of June and July, the unit was deployed in the East, where PzJgAbt 1389 was able to destroy 24 enemy tanks, with a total loss of three StuG IV. Of the remaining vehicles, only three were still operational, one of which had its availability limited due to a defective engine. The report describes the condition of the assault guns as poor. Due to improper running-in, the engines were overstressed; the commander suspected the inexperienced young drivers were the cause. The widened *Ostketten* (east tracks), which certainly brought advantages in mud and snow, proved to be too heavy for the steering gear and final drives. To avoid further losses, the 40cm standard tracks were ordered to be put back on and the damaged engines replaced.

A group of *Fallschirmjäger* (paratroopers) being transported on a JgdPz IV in service with *Fallschirmjäger-Panzerdivision* (FSchmPzDiv – Parachute Tank Division) Hermann Göring. The vehicle would have been fitted with *Panzerschürzen*, but these have been ripped off, leaving only the badly damaged brackets.

The report went on to describe such a dramatic shortage of fuel that the supply had to be ensured by specially allocated vehicles.

By the end of August, no more StuG IVs were available: three had to be written off as a total loss and the remaining four were taken to the *Heimat-Instandsetzung* (local repair depot) in Riga with serious damage.

The StuGAbt 1389, now an established unit. A month later, the unit was sent back to Mielau ready to take delivery of more assault guns. The new vehicles reached the division in the course of November. Now fully operational again, the division immediately lost an assault gun in the swampy terrain south of Riga.

In his report, the commander describes the inadequacy of the RSO tractors, which repeatedly proved unsuitable for towing the 7.5cm PaK. In view of the difficult terrain in Courland, the StuG IV was also criticized due to its lack of all-terrain mobility, which made it impossible for the division to engage in mobile combat.

In the meantime, the tank crews had been able to gain valuable experience in combat. In accordance with current regulations, the division had set up a grenadier escort platoon, which, armed with MP 43 assault rifles, was responsible for protecting the assault guns.

The reinforced repair platoon, which was established provisionally, worked reliably and smoothly. Conversely, the assignment of the *Bergepanzer* III armoured recovery vehicle was not a success, as it was too light to tow the heavier assault guns. Also, the vehicles were mechanically unreliable, since they were built on refurbished PzKpfw III chassis. As with the assault guns, the drive components remained delicate, which caused frequent breakdowns.

Due to the fierce fighting, the number of wounded crewmen within StuGAbt 1389 – commanders, gunners, loaders and drivers – rose to a critical level. Replacement personnel could not be provided and nor could vital spare parts such as final drive units.

The last available strength report was submitted on 1 March 1945. The commander reported a dramatic drop in combat strength. Of the established strength of 14 assault guns, only four were still operational and two others were in short-term repair.

The loss of good commanders and specific crew had a very negative effect on their deployment. Two months later, the war was over.

The assault gun concept was copied by the Russians in World War II, probably as a result of their own experiences with the StuG III.

A New *Sturmgeschütz*

In 1943, mass production of the new PzKpfw V Panther tank began. Initially, one of the two PzAbt in each PzDiv was to be equipped with the new tank,

while the other battalion continued to be equipped with PzKpfw IV. In the long term, the PzKpfw IV was to be completely replaced. As a direct consequence of these plans, production of the PzKpfw IV by VOMAG at Plauen was discontinued in May 1944.

As early as September 1942, the HWa had commissioned the company to develop a modernized successor to the StuG based on the PzKpfw IV chassis. Initial wooden mock-ups showed a flat vehicle with a superstructure fabricated from acutely sloped plates. From the beginning of development, it was planned to mount the 7.5cm KwK 42 L/70, as used in the PzKpfw V Panther, but due to technical problems, it was replaced by the 7.5cm PaK39, a variant of the 7.5cm L/48.

The planned introduction of a new unit chassis with six larger rubber-saving running wheels on three bogies was to be discarded, as was the use of an SSG 77 transmission from the PzKpfw III as it proved inferior to the SSG 76 (PzKpfw IV) in terms of reliability.

For reasons of standardization, it was now decided to use the chassis of the PzKpfw IV for this vehicle, since production of the PzKpfw III was to be discontinued in the near future. But these plans, like many others, were quickly discarded. Both the StuG III and the StuG IV remained in production until the end of the war.

The Panzer IV/70(V) prototype was presented to Adolf Hitler on 6 July 1944. Impressed by the strong frontal armour and the powerful 7.5cm PaK 42 L/70, he described the vehicle as one of the 'best solutions of the war'.

Right: The first production JgdPz IV were fitted with a muzzle brake, but not only was it found to be unnecessary, it also raised a large cloud when the gun fired. Consequently, many units decided to remove the item.

Below: This JgdPz IV was hit on the side at the level of the first support roller and burnt out. Note the threading on the gun barrel where the muzzle brake was fitted.

Left: A devastating explosion has lifted the heavily armoured superstructure on this JgdPz IV off the chassis.

Below: The excessive weight of the JgdPz IV overloaded the transmission, which resulted in many of the type being abandoned with only minor defects. If it could not be repaired or recovered by field engineers, the crew was under orders to destroy it with demolition charges.

Sturmgeschütz-Abteilung (in PzJgAbt)
Ten or 14 StuG according to KStN 1149 dated 1 February 1944
Optional equipment with StuG III, StuG IV or PzJg IV

Gruppe Führer

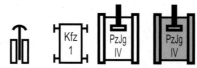

Gefechtskompanie

1.Zug   **2.Zug**   **3.Zug**

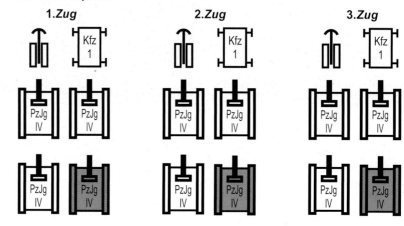

Kfz-Inst-Gruppe

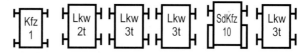

Bergetrupp   Gepäcktross

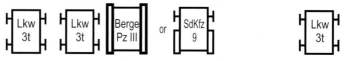

Gefechtstross

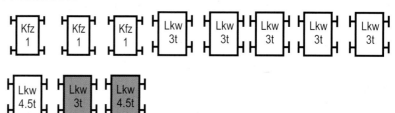

Optional provision for
StuGAbt with 14 StuGs

As late as autumn 1943, Karl Saur, an office director working for the new armaments minister Albert Speer, determined that the PzKpfw IV was to be used as the *Endlösung* (final solution) for all light armoured vehicles. Like many 'final solutions', this decision was quickly rendered obsolete by the developments on the battlefront.

Where the 7.5cm StuK 40 in the StuG was fitted on a pedestal-type mounting, a space-saving, ball-type mounting, bolted directly to the sloping superstructure was designed for the 7.5cm PaK 39 L/48. Initially, the 'new assault gun' was called the *leichter Panzerjager* (le JgdPz – light tank hunter/destroyer) IV, but this was soon changed to JgdPz IV.

The sloping superstructure was intended to remedy fundamental weaknesses of the assault gun. Like the hull, the superstructure was 60mm thick at the front and, being inclined at 45–50 degrees, a high level of protection was achieved. Side protection was also improved to 40mm, which made the vehicle safe from the feared 14.5mm PTRS and PTRD anti-tank rifles used by the Red Army. It was originally planned to fit an assault gun-type commander's cupola with various vision devices and an MG 34 that could be operated from inside the vehicle, but both were dropped for unknown reasons. Possibly, this was once again influenced by economic and supply difficulties.

Instead, the much less elaborate *Nahverteidigungswaffe* (close-in defence weapon), which could fire smoke or 2.6cm fragmentation grenades, was fitted. Presumably due to a lack of materials, this was not available in sufficient quantities; on most vehicles, the opening was covered by a steel plate.

A coating of Zimmerit anti-magnetic paste was applied on all production JgdPz IV until September 1944. Ultimately, this useless practice was ended on all armoured vehicles.

Below: A shell fired from a Red Army anti-tank gun has hit and entered the superstructure of this JgdPz IV and, surprisingly, not detonated. The lack of threading on the muzzle indicates that the 7.5cm PaK 39 was never fitted with a muzzle brake.

Left: The 116.PzDiv was deployed to Normandy in response to the D-Day landings on 6 June 1944. A month later, their PzJgAbt was issued with 21 JgdPz IV but the majority of these were lost as German forces retreated. After the unit was almost completely wiped out, it was issued with more Panzer IV/70, followed by a number of assault guns in December.

Below: The rough texture of the Zimmerit anti-magnetic paste made it difficult to apply markings. Here, an area has been sanded smooth to allow the application of a tactical symbol and vehicle number.

Above: December 1944: A line of incomplete Panzer IV/70 (A) at Nibelungenwerk, St Valentin, Austria. The sign laments that the vehicles cannot be completed due to a lack of parts – an indication of the deteriorating situation in the German armaments industry.

Right: While VOMAG designed its own specialized hull for the Panzer IV/70(V), Nibelungenwerk was forced to utilize an unchanged PzKpfw IV hull. Consequently, the Panzer IV/70(A) had a considerably higher superstructure.

The prototype of the Panzer IV/70 (A) still had vertical side walls on the lower part of the superstructure. Since the weight of the type was 27,000kg, some 1,500kg heavier than the VOMAG version, the first four running wheels were of solid steel type.

Compared with the StuG IV, the IV was more powerful. The combat weight dropped to 24,000kg due to the reduction of the front armour from 80mm to 60mm. This made the vehicle almost 2,000kg lighter than the StuG IV, with corresponding improvements in mobility, particularly steering.

In the course of production, as with all German armoured vehicles, various changes were successively introduced. For example, in May 1944, the front armour was reinforced to 80mm, which eliminated the weight advantage.

The reasons why Krupp-Gruson did not take the superior JgdPz IV into production instead of the StuG IV remain unknown. Presumably, it was necessary to start manufacturing as quickly as possible. A costly changeover would certainly have resulted in a longer delay. The army, which was severely pressed on three battlefronts in 1944, did not have this time.

Allocation

From March 1944 onwards, the le JgdPz IV were largely assigned to the PzJgAbt in PzDiv and PzGrenDiv according to a certain key. The basic form of organization was regulated by KStN 1149. But the first version, published on 1 February 1944, still showed the designation: *Sturmgeschütz-Abteilung auf Panzerjäger-Abteilung zu 10 oder 14 Geschützen* (assault gun battalion in tank

Above: A tank destroyer company, equipped with new vehicles, on combat manoeuvres at *Panzerjäger-Schule* (anti-tank school), Mielau. After a short training period, the unit and their vehicles would be deployed to the battlefront.

Left: The installation of the powerful 7.5cm PaK 42 L/70 gun in the JgdPz IV was a logical step that could be achieved without any major modifications. This is a prototype of the Panzer IV/70(V), which was based on a JgdPz IV, but with 60mm front armour.

Left: A burnt-out US Army M4A1 Sherman lies abandoned, as does a mine-damaged JgdPz IV, while Allied forces advance through the Meurthe-Moselle region in north-eastern France.

hunter/destroyer battalion with ten or 14 guns).

Thus the *Abteilung* was actually a *Kompanie* (Kp – company) that could initially be equipped with either assault guns (StuG III or StuG IV) or the 7.5cm PaK 39-armed JgdPz 38, known as *Hetzer* (hunter), although the JgdPz IV was also issued depending on availability.

The PzJg divisions in a PzDiv was to have two companies of ten JgdPz IV each, and another for the battalion commander. The PzJg detachments in a PzGrenDiv were to have two companies each with JgdPz IV, and a further three for the detachment staff. There were a number of exceptions to this rule. For example, the *Fallschirmjäger-Panzerdivision* (FSchPzDiv – parachute tank division) Hermann Göring, received a total of 31 JgdPz IV for its III.Div.

PzJgAbt 196 was one of the units assigned JgdPz IV in company strength. The assignment took place at the end of August in Mielau, after which the unit was transferred with 96.InfDiv, its parent unit, to the Eastern Front, where it was involved in heavy fighting.

On 30 September 1944, the commander of the 2./PzJgAbt 196 submitted a field report:

The roof on the superstructure of a Panzer IV/70 (V). The *Zielenfernrohr* (ZF – telescopic sight) 1a was attached to a rail that allowed a commander to track a target.

A knocked-out tank destroyer. An anti-tank shell has destroyed the idler wheel during the fighting near Lake Balaton, Hungary, in 1945. Note the crew has attached spare track links to the left side of the superstructure as extra protection.

The company was reorganized and retrained on JgdPz (old) (*) at Mielau and has been in action on the Eastern Front since 25 August 1944. The company gained its first combat experience with this weapon in defensive battles and local counterattacks. The missions were conducted in confusing, mountainous terrain with limited operational possibilities.

As a result of the high losses to friendly infantry, sections of the front often had to be defended without infantry protection, with the terrain precluding any mobile fighting. This gave the enemy the opportunity to take the JgdPz positions under fire of his combined artillery and mortars, without them having the chance to avoid the fire by moving into alternative positions. Nevertheless, all attacks during the day could be repelled. At night, enemy infantry came close to the defenders and had to be repulsed by the crews in close combat. This succeeded because the Russian infantry did not have the necessary attacking spirit. The use of the JgdPz IV as dug-in anti-tank guns is contrary to their intended use and will ultimately lead to unnecessary losses. However, this approach had to be ordered and carried out due to necessity.

During the counterattacks, it became apparent that the tank destroyer, in addition to its firepower, had a significant effect on enemy morale that should not be underestimated. Often the enemy infantrymen took flight, leaving all weapons behind. However, this initial success could not be extended due to the difficult terrain and the lack of support from our infantry. Special attention should be paid to the use of the machine gun, with which good success was achieved. However,

Below: A white camouflaged JgdPz IV in service with the PzJgAbt of 19.PzDiv. At the beginning of 1945, the battalion was engaged in defensive combat on the Vistula Front. Note the vehicle carries a 7.92mm MG 42 in an improvised mounting.

Left: Two PzKpfw V Panther medium tanks and a Panzer IV/70 (V) from PzBrig 105 have been abandoned by their crews after being fired on by Allied ground-attack aircraft.

Below: A Panzer IV/70(V) travels through a village in Poland as German forces continue their rapid retreat on the Eastern Front. Note the SdKfz 251 *mittlerer Schützenpanzerwagen* (m SPW – medium armoured personnel carrier) for the always-present supporting PzGren.

Heavily camouflaged with foliage, a JgdPz IV moves through a village in Normandy after the D-Day landings. Whenever possible, German armour was moved between dusk and dawn to avoid being spotted by Allied ground-attack aircraft.

a number of machine gunners, who are also loaders, were wounded or killed (**).

In combat in built-up areas and in wooded terrain, the *Jäger* is helpless without infantry protection. It can be destroyed very easily by anti-tank guns from the flank and rear or by close-combat fighters. Our infantry does not, all too often, understand this fact. Despite the fact that the tank destroyer should only be deployed in cooperation with grenadiers (***), this tactic could not always be enforced because the grenadier units suffered very high losses. Deployment without infantry protection could have led to the destruction of the JgdPz IV if the enemy infantry had been good.

During combat against tanks in villages, enemy types with their rotating turrets were inevitably at an advantage, but it was nevertheless possible, in cooperation with our infantry, to destroy every enemy tank without any losses. Even in open terrain, almost all tanks encountered in the company's sector could be knocked out. These successes could be achieved because it was possible to let the enemy become bogged down and because the enemy drove his attacks with closed hatches and thus without sufficient observation.

Especially in unclear terrain, the commander must observe from the open hatch of his vehicle in order to monitor the battlefield, even at the risk of being wounded. Because he is in a better position to observe the enemy, he can also take the fire fight to a numerically superior enemy tank force.

The company was able to destroy 14 tanks, mainly the T-34. We scored hits on the front armour and also the sides. In both cases, the effect of our gun was devastating. All the tanks hit rapidly caught fire. Own losses: Two JgdPz IV were hit and immobilized by anti-tank guns, and another two were damaged. All vehicles could be recovered.

From a technical point of view, the following difficulties and shortcomings arose:

The Panzer IV/70 (V) was decidedly front-heavy due to the 80mm armour and the weight of the 7.5cm PaK 42 L/70 gun. Steering movements, particularly over soft terrain, often overloaded the delicate *Seitenvorgelage* (final drive) units, which would fail and leave the vehicle immobilized.

Left: The supply of ammunition and other materials became more problematic as German forces rapidly lost ground to Red Army forces advancing from the East and Allied forces attacking from the West. The constant shortage of fuel forced many crews to abandon and destroy their vehicles.

Below: Celebrating victory: Russian officers and civilians on a badly damaged Panzer IV//70 (A), captured by the Red Army. The tactical number, 929, indicates that it was in service with a tank division.

Tank drivers and tank mechanics had, for the most part, only been trained for a short period. Consequently, they had to gain their experience during front-line operations. Added to this is the difficult terrain, which places particularly high demands on vehicles and drivers. The winding roads, the rugged terrain and the fact that the *Jäger* were equipped with *Ostketten* (****) had a detrimental effect. The engine is powerful but delicate. Despite correct maintenance, two engines had to be replaced after 600km. The gearbox seems to be very susceptible; three failed after 500km and had to undergo major repairs. The wear and tear on the Hardy discs (*****) is very high. A lot of effort and sacrificial maintenance work is required for the parking and steering brakes. Even after the most accurate and careful adjustment, steering difficulty and other problems often appear after only a

This Panzer IV/70 (V) was apparently stopped by a hit on the right drive wheel. The vehicle shows the *Licht-und-Schatten Tarnung* (light-and-shadow camouflage), also known as the ambush scheme.

short distance. Hot running brakes frequently cause shoes and adjusting bands to break. The running gear is satisfactory, although on hard-surfaced road, the rubber tyres peel off the running wheels.

The recovery and towing of immobilized *Jäger* poses particular difficulties. Since the company is not in possession of an operational towing vehicle, an immobilized *Jäger* had to be towed by another. In the process, the towing vehicles often suffered damage as well. Towing by the recovery company is associated with a serious loss of time, as the vehicles are not always available. It would therefore be in the interest of operational readiness to assign the company its own SdKfz 7 half-track tractor. Repair work also causes difficulties, as the company is attached to an infantry division that is not in possession of the necessary repair services.

Field engineers have assembled a simple crane over the engine bay of a StuG IV to remove the Maybach HL 120TRM. This same engine was used to power all assault guns and tank destroyers that used a PzKpfw IV chassis.

(*) Armed with PaK 39 L/48.

(**) This is understandable, as the MG had no armour protection when used outside the vehicle.

(***) This has been emphasized over and over again in all the operational regulations.

(****) The east tracks, widened on one side, were developed for use in the mud and snow of the *Ostfront* (East Front). At 55cm, they were significantly wider than the standard 40cm track.

(*****) The Hardy discs or Giubo coupling were used to connect the Cardan shaft to the transmission.

The November issue of the *Nachrichtenblatt der Panzertruppe* (Bulletin of the Armoured Forces) describes the deployment of an unknown PzJgAbt in the East:

> The JgdPz IV fully proved itself against fire from Russian 7.62cm anti-tank guns and heavy mortars. The 21 in the division did not suffer any losses due to enemy action despite several hits from these weapons. The task of securing our units

Left: Whenever possible, German units moved their armoured vehicles (here an assault gun from a tank destroyer company) by rail to avoid mechanical wear.

Below: Belgium, January 1945: A JgdPz IV lies abandoned on a country road near Cherain, a small town north of Bastogne.

Camouflaged with whitewash paint, this StuG IV is fitted with 55cm *Ostketten,* which were 15cm wider than the standard tracks and reduced ground pressure considerably. However, many field reports state that these tracks frequently caused final drive units to fail.

against enemy tanks and supporting the grenadiers in infantry combat could be fulfilled in all cases. In offensive combat, it was also possible to temporarily hold large sectors without the support from other units. Subordination to smaller units than the regiment easily leads to a fragmented deployment and ultimately to unnecessary losses. It is therefore necessary that the leader of a JgdPz IV unit enforces a united deployment by clear orders and does not let the leadership out of his hands.

All too often, orders were given from a higher authority to lead operational JgdPz IV into battle and deploy those that were no longer mobile as stationary PaK. The implementation of this order was bound to lead to the loss of these tanks. For this reason, the commander of a JgdPz IV unit must use all his energy to point out that the use of an immobilized JgdPz IV is futile, since it cannot be steered without the engine running. Deprived of mobility, it becomes easy prey for the enemy and must be blown up. It should also be pointed out that most mechanical damage can be repaired in hours or a few days. The JgdPz IV in question will then be fully operational again, whereas it will be lost if such orders are carried out. A responsible unit commander must therefore employ all means to recover any non-operational tank for repair.

The deployment of JgdPz IV in unclear terrain and without surveillance by grenadiers often leads to the loss of a tank due to the approach of enemy close-combat teams.

The permanent attachment of a grenadier unit to a tank destroyer/assault gun battalion has proven to be excellent. The reinforced grenadier company attached to the battalion had already fully adapted to escorting and monitoring the JgdPz IV after the first battle. It was also able to conduct independent attacks and counterattacks with limited objectives under the fire protection of the JgdPz IV. During assault missions, many enemy heavy weapons detected were damaged or abandoned, but could not be captured by the JgdPz IV.

The engagement of infantry targets with explosive grenades, which are used by the grenadiers because of their effect on enemy morale, cannot be reconciled with the low ammunition supply. The front-line MG performs excellently at all target ranges if the commander provides tight fire control. The use of smoke and anti-personnel grenades must be limited to deployment against recognized heavy weapons and whole units, and for self-defence. Reserves of all types of ammunition must be retained. It is proposed that, in the JgdPz IV, the defensive grenades be retained in the holders to the left of the commander, and that one box each of belted MG, pistol, and MP ammunition, as well as five *Stielhandgranate* [stick hand grenade], be stowed in the fighting compartment.

The deployment of le JgdPz IV units without sufficient repair services and recovery resources leads to the unnecessary loss of a tank. The independent deployment of such units or an individual tank is therefore to be rejected.

Street fighting in Warsaw: A JgdPz IV, in service with the PzJgAbt attached to 5.SS-PzDiv Wiking, provides supporting fire to German infantry as they strive to overrun an enemy-held position. (Getty)

Italy in 1944: The crew of this 8.8cm FlaK 36 has painted 16 'victory' rings on the barrel of their gun. The JgdPz IV is in service with the PzJgAbt of 26.PzDiv.

Above: A Panzer IV/70 (V) armed with a 7.5cm PaK 42 L/70 smoulders in a village street after a shell fired from a Red Army T-34/85 penetrated the 40mm side armour.

Right: A relatively large number of Panzer IV/70(V) were deployed during the Battle of the Bulge: 16 December 1944 to 25 January 1945. This abandoned vehicle belonged to s PzJgAbt 560, which was attached to the 12.SS-PzDiv Hitlerjugend in December 1944.

In unclear situations, such as those during the fighting around Baranowicze and subsequent retreat movements, damaged armoured vehicles of other units were often recovered using those roads blocked by supply transports. As these were too slow, the recovery teams came under enemy attack and many vehicles had to be blown up. In such cases, it proved expedient to deploy repair services near a railway and tow damaged tanks there under the leadership of an energetic and prudent officer (made mobile by wheeled vehicle), so that rapid loading was possible in the event of the enemy making contact. In this way, the battalion has recovered 17 JgdPz, three PzKpfw IV and one Hungarian [*Turán*] tank by railway before these damaged tanks were reached by the enemy.

Through appropriate training and under the supervision of an experienced officer, it has been possible in all cases to remove valuable equipment from vehicles being prepared for demolition, even under the heaviest enemy fire. Often, the crews achieved this despite being surrounded by the enemy. In one instance, the crews of two JgdPz IV, working at night, removed radios, converters and other equipment and carried it back through enemy positions after preparing demolition charges. The dismantling of the equipment, as well as the preparation for demolition, must be included as part of crew training.

Medical care for the severely wounded in moving battles proved difficult, especially at night. The division did not have any wheeled or half-track *Krankenkraftwagen* [ambulances]. Consequently, the following is proposed: During combat activity at night, an approximately 1m-deep trench is dug under the commander's tank, lined with canvas and covered laterally against light escaping, so that the medical officer can take care of the wounded.

The GenInsp d PzTrp commented on the report:

The report shows that the le JgdPz IV, due to the effectiveness of its weapon and armour, can fulfil the main tasks of anti-tank combat and infantry support. However, it is a prerequisite that it is used according to its concept – mobility and great firepower. Consequently, such an essential vehicle requires careful maintenance, to keep it at operational readiness.

On 18 January 1945, the commander of 1./PzJgAbt 20 (20.PzGrenDiv) filed a dramatic combat report. The unit was issued with JgdPz IV armed with the PaK 39 L/48 from the stock held by *Panzerjäger-Schule* at *Truppenübungsplatz* (troop training area) Mielau (Młaṃwa) in Poland, and apparently all were in poor condition. Immediately after taking over and with only one day of training, the PzJgAbt had to intervene, as part of a combat group, in the defensive battles north of Mielau, independently of the parent unit, 20.PzGrenDiv.

16 January 1945

According to orders, Herr Drechsler, head of *Arbeitsstab* [mission staff] at *Panzerjäger-Schule* Mielau, is to issue 12 JgdPz IV to Major Goldammer when he becomes *Kampf-Kommandant* [battle commander] of 1./PzJgAbt 20.

17 January 1945

The 12 JgdPz IV and two StuG IV ordered on 16 January have been transferred. The tanks are of an older type and have a considerable number of mechanical defects. The radio and the intercom system are not in order. The commander's tank lacks the mounting and antenna for the Fu 8 radio. The location and the urgency of the

This JgdPz IV was abandoned when the Red Army captured the fortress of Königsberg, Kaliningrad, in 1945. Externally undamaged, the vehicle still has a coating of Zimmerit anti-magnetic paste. Note the conical armoured cover over the pistol port adjacent to the mantlet.

situation do not permit the installation of this equipment. The combat squadron and the few specialists remaining with the company are working diligently to make these fighting vehicles ready for combat. All tank guards, the tank radio control room and the recovery team are at the *Panzerjäger-Schule,* at Neuhammer, Silesia, to improve their knowledge. The company commander requested by telephone the accelerated deployment of these specialists to Mielau. They did not arrive in time.

At 09:00hrs, the company, under the command of the school and led by the training officer *Oberleutnant* Ostermann, moves to Zarnowo to practise at firing range No. 21.

At 14:00hrs, the company commander receives the mission order from Major Goldammer.

Enemy situation: The enemy has broken through our positions on a broad front between Nasielsk and Zichenau [Ciechanów] and is advancing with strong tank and infantry forces towards the Praschnitz-Mielau [Przasnysz-Mlawa] highway. It is expected that the enemy will reach the area during the course of the day.

1./PzJgAbt 20 takes up position in the area hard east of Robierz and reconnoitres firing positions in and around the woodland southeast of Robierz in order to monitor PzJgAbt 4, which is deployed with about 120 infantrymen.

At 15:45hrs, the deployment has taken place as ordered. At 18:00hrs, a briefing is made by the commander of PzGrenRgt 30. Our attack is planned for 08:00hrs and we are to take enemy positions 3km south of Grudusk. On the right, Fusilier Regiment GD, on the left PzGrenRgt 30. Supporting the attack will be I./PzRgt GD with 24 PzKpfw V Panthers on the right and two JgdPz IV companies from the *Panzerjäger-Schule* Mielau on the left.

At 24:00hrs, the enemy attacked Grudusk with strong forces from the south-east and south. We repelled their infantry and occupied the place during the night. By chance, the company learns from elements of ArtRgt GD in Robierz that the division's counterattack, scheduled for 18 January, will not take place.

A crewman guides the driver of a pre-production Panzer IV/70(V) as he positions the vehicle on a *Reichautobahn* (state highway) in preparation for an inspection by the Führer. The port for a second MG, above the driver's visor, was omitted on series production vehicles.

18 January 1945

At 14:00hrs, warning posts detect enemy tank movements to the southeast of Grudusk after hearing loud track noises. The company takes up alert firing positions. The company commander informs the platoon leader of the situation and then orders us to tune our radios. He then drives with the leader of 1.Zug to Kolaki to take command of PzJgAbt 4.

Even before the *vorgeschobener Beobachter* [VB – forward observer] team from the artillery takes up its position, 1./PzJgAbt 20 detects a single enemy tank of the Sherman type. At 08:00hrs, the tank attack rolls towards Kolaki and Robierz; some 35 to 40 tanks, mostly type Sherman and some T-43(*), and all with mounted infantry. A strong motorized infantry battalion follows the attack.

At 08:05hrs, the company opened fire – from concealed positions, in the area overgrown with bushes – on the enemy tanks travelling at around 35kph. In 20 minutes, 14 enemy tanks (one T-43, 13 Sherman) are knocked out and left burning. Escorting infantry and disembarked crews are cut down by high-explosive mortar fire and also machine gun fire from the tanks. The attack comes to a halt in front of our own position. Enemy tanks driving through a depression quickly turn and flee. The dangerous tank attack on Mielau has been shattered.

Note: Only ten of the 14 vehicles at the school were roadworthy and ready for action. Only one old *Bergepanzer* III [armoured recovery vehicle] was available to the company. Of the ten le JgdPz IV that went into action, only six fired properly. The others had damage to the electric firing circuit, the range calculating machines and aiming devices.

(*) German sources often refer to the T-34/85 as T-43; presumably German intelligence misinterpreted reports of the actual T-43 prototype.

On 6 February 1945, the commander of PzJgAbt 53 (5. PzDiv) submitted his monthly strength report. From the established strength of 21 JgdPz IV only 14 were still available, half of which were undergoing repairs (long-term over three weeks). Of two *Bergepanzer* III, only one remained, and this was also under repair. The commander reported on the difficulties of the operation:

The very mobile combat operations of the last few weeks have shown that, from a mechanical point of view, the JgdPz IV in no way meets the requirements for these types of operations. Even with only minor marching stress, a large number of the type failed due to damage to the final drive units, gearbox and engine. With the often dispersed deployment of the division and the roads completely clogged with civilian convoys, the few towing resources available were not sufficient to recover all damaged vehicles in time during almost daily marches. Subsequently, of the 14

The five-man crew of a JgdPz IV: The screw thread on the gun barrel, for fitting a muzzle brake, indicates that this is an early production vehicle. The *Panzerschürzen* are of the later, hinged type, allowing easier access to the running gear for repair or maintenance.

total losses in the battalion, only five were lost in combat, mainly due to enemy action. The rest all had to be blown up due to a lack of recovery vehicles and in order to not let them fall into enemy hands.

Repairing any damaged JgdPz IV was impossible during the daily retreat movements and the resulting changes to the location of maintenance services.

With great effort and using all available forces, the battalion succeeded in towing 11 damaged JgdPz IV and three PaK-Sfl to PzInstKp 657 (by rail) at Zinten; the rest of the battalion was deployed in the fortress of Königsberg. The six JgdPz IV, which were ready for action again, were individually issued to four different infantry or *Volksgrenadier* divisions by order of the army group.

Following the experience gained so far, such a deployment of individual tank destroyers to units that do not have the necessary repair services and towing vehicles, and have no experience whatsoever of operating the JgdPz IV, will inevitably lead to the total loss of all vehicles within a very short time.

Despite these difficulties, the battalion destroyed 87 enemy tanks and 43 anti-tank guns during the period between 14 January and 2 February 1945 with an average of only seven operational JgdPz IV.

A month later, the commander reported:

The spare parts situation can still be described as poor. In particular, there is a lack of hubs and items for repairing the *Umlaufgetriebe* [planetary gears] in a *Seitenvorgelege* [final drive unit].

Panzer IV/70(V)

The production of JgdPz IV L/48 ended in November 1944, after 769 vehicles had been delivered.

In the meantime, the problems concerning the installation of the 7.5cm PaK 42 L/70 had been solved. The gun mantlet had to be redesigned, and the ammunition holders were adapted for longer cartridges and ammunition stowage was reduced to 60 (some sources state 55) shells.

Hitler, who was shown a prototype of the vehicle on the occasion of his birthday, on 20 April 1944, immediately ordered the greatest possible expansion of production.

This began in August 1944 and approximately 940 vehicles had been completed by the end of the war. This almost met the requirements of the HWa, which called for 2,020 JgdPz IV of both types in the production programme by April 1944.

The vehicle was designated Panzer(V); the 'V' indicates that it was manufactured by VOMAG.

The weight of the Pz IV/70 had increased significantly (25,800kg compared with 24,000kg) due to increasing the front armour to 80mm and the installation of the long-barrelled gun. As a result, the front-heaviness, which had already been noted during trials, was increased. Since the front running wheels were subjected to heavy steering movements, which put undue stress on the rubber tyres, they were soon replaced by rubber-saving steel wheels.

The first available Panzer IV/70(V) went to the newly established *Panzerbrigaden* (PzBrig – tank brigades) in July 1944. These ten units (PzBrig 101 to PzBrig 110) were to be deployed quickly to hot spots as highly mobile independent tank units. Each brigade had three tank companies, each issued with 11 PzKpfw V Panther tanks, a tank destroyer company with 11 Panzer IV/70(V), and also a PzGren battalion. The concept did not work well in practice, partly because the brigades lacked an integrated artillery component. Five were deployed on the Western Front and the Eastern Front. After a few

These Panzer IV/70 (V) are from the last series. Due to a lack of materiel, neither side skirts nor the armour protection for the engine compartment were mounted. Note the two front running wheels have been replaced by rubber-saving ones.

months, in October/November 1944, the units were disbanded and used to reinforce a number of other units.

In this context, the monthly report from 17.PzDiv, dated 1 September 1944, is interesting:

> The mood of the troops has suffered due to the hard, uninterrupted deployment of the last four weeks. The crews are physically and mentally over-stressed. A few days of rest and the immediate influence of the commanders and his officers would quickly bring about a noticeable improvement. The troops have often unambiguously criticized that the newly established PzBrig have all the tried and tested weapons that the front-line troops have been lacking for months. The men often found that the inexperienced units left their valuable equipment on the battlefield, where most fell into the hands of the Russians.

Subsequently, the Panzer IV/70(V) were allocated in the same way as the JgdPz IV to the tank destroyer divisions in some PzDiv, PzGrenDiv and SS-PzDiv, sometimes as full equipment (21 or 31), and often in the course of replacement deliveries in smaller quantities. Furthermore, four independent heavy PzJgAbt received different quantities of these vehicles as part of their very mixed equipment.

At the end of January 1945, 14 Panzer IV/70(V) were assigned to the 25.PzDiv. The vehicles were assigned to the 6.Kp of PzRgt 9.

An entry in diary of the platoon leader reveals interesting details:

At the end of January 1945, the company received 14 Pz IV/70(V) tanks at the Neuhammer military training area near Sagan (Silesia). The vehicles were briefly checked, camouflaged for winter use, then test driven, and the guns tried and adjusted. The new JgdPz were the best armoured vehicles I ever sat or fought in during the war. Especially in the anti-tank role, which had absolute priority in the last months of the war.

We were first deployed in the last days of January. After numerous enemy contacts, our unit was ordered to hold a bridgehead on the Oder, near Stettin. The platoon was assigned to reinforce an infantry unit and conduct reconnaissance.

From 16 March 1945, the Russians began preparations for an attack with heavy artillery fire and attacks by waves of up to 60 ground-attack bombers. It was the strongest concentration of fire I have ever experienced on the Eastern Front. We immediately pulled in our *Scherenfernrohr* [SF – scissors-type periscope] and MG and closed all hatches; the shell splinters flying around could only scratch our armour. Around 09:00hrs, we learned that the Russians had assembled a large number of tanks in front of our forward infantry lines. After radio calls to our division and the regiment, we finally learned from an infantry dispatcher that the rest of our company and division were already attacking.

The action was delayed by the terrain being cratered by bombs and shells. At exactly 01:00hrs, the artillery fire abruptly ceased and a deathly silence surrounded us, and then, from our foxholes and machine gun positions, flares rose into the sky, and the enemy attacked.

The first T-34/85 and SU-85 rolled into view of our *Jagdpanzer*, which were waiting in covered firing positions. We saw the first flashes of light from hits on the leading T-34s, which began to smoke shortly afterwards. Then, five to eight more enemy tanks appeared behind them, were also hit and burned immediately. The same happened with all the other attacking enemy tanks. Every shot from our guns was a hit. We had not assigned our oldest and most experienced corporals and other NCOs as gunners without good reason, since they rarely missed their target. After some 30min of firefighting, a strong formation of T-34s attempted to bypass us and attack from the right flank. We had fired almost all our ammunition when additional *Jagdpanzer* behind us and to the side opened fire on the attacking Russians. The rest of the battalion had joined us and supported our bitterly fought defensive battle against the overwhelming Russian formations.

Our *Jagdpanzer* received numerous hits during this engagement, which lasted into the afternoon. However, we remained in action until the last surviving Russian tank had withdrawn. As the enemy vehicles were retreating, we received another heavy hit, this time on the final drive, which immobilized our vehicle. We waited for our comrades from the *Panzer-Bergestaffel* [amoured recovery squadron], who towed us to the other bank of the Oder.

Panzer IV/70(A)

Even before VOMAG began production of the Panzer IV/70, the HWa was instructed in June 1944 to carry out investigations into maintaining the combat capability of the PzKpfw IV.

Compared with the Russian standard tank T-34/76, the PzKpfw IV did not perform very well. The T-34/85, which was arriving in ever larger numbers, was far superior in a direct comparison. Due to the poor manufacturing infrastructure, production of the tank could never be switched to the PzKpfw V Panther; as the expected loss of new tanks would have led to a crisis at the front.

Attempts to increase the firepower of the PzKpfw IV by fitting the 7.5cm KwK 42 L/70 proved technically impracticable. On the other hand, VOMAG successfully switched production to the JgdPz IV as early as January.

A similar conversion at the last remaining manufacturer of the PzKpfw IV, the Nibelungenwerk, proved impossible for unknown reasons. It seems conceivable that the disadvantages of a casemate-type tank in service with tank divisions were considered too severe.

The crew of this Panzer IV/70 (V) has followed orders and used a demolition charge, which has destroyed the entire left-hand side of the superstructure. The white number was applied by Russian clearing squads.

The 1.85m overall height of the Panzer IV/70 (V) mounting a 7.5cm PaK 42 L/70 made it ideal for fighting from a camouflaged position, but any offensive deployment was severely limited due to a lack of mobility.

It was now decided to adapt the superstructure of the Panzer IV/70(V) to the hull of the PzKpfw IV. The development contract was issued to Alkett, the specialist for tracked assault and self-propelled guns. A direct mounting of the superstructure was not possible, because the fuel tank in the rear of the hull severely limited the elevation of the 7.5cm PaK 42 L/70. This resulted in a new superstructure, some 35cm higher, being developed.

The result was an extremely high vehicle, and the weight increased to 28,000kg, which greatly affected the driving characteristics. The front load became even higher. In order to protect the running wheels from damage, the front four were replaced by rubber-saving steel wheels.

Assignments

The Nibelungenwerk was now to convert part of the PzKpfw IV production to the new assault gun/tank destroyer. The vehicle was designated Panzer IV/70(A) – the 'A' indicates Alkett.

The first available vehicles were assigned in varying numbers to six PzDiv

Performance: 7.5cm StuK 42 L/70

Usage	Pz IV/70(V) and Pz IV/70(A)
Calibre	7.5cm
Barrel length	5,255mm
Calibre length	L/70
Rate of fire	Ten rounds per minute
Barrel life span	2,000 to 3,000 rounds

Ammunition

7.5cm SprGr 42

Muzzle velocity	700mps
Range (maximum)	10,000m

7.5cm PzGr 39/42

Muzzle velocity	935mps
Penetration at 100m	138mm
Penetration at 500m	124mm
Penetration at 1,000m	111mm
Penetration at 1,500m	99mm
Penetration at 2,000m	88mm

7.5cm PzGr 40/42

Muzzle velocity	1,120mps
Penetration at 100m	194mm
Penetration at 500m	174mm
Penetration at 1,000m	150mm
Penetration at 1,500m	127mm
Penetration at 2,000m	106mm

on the Eastern Front. The JgdPz were to support the PzKpfw IV with their long-range weapons. The PzRgt Großdeutschland was to receive a complete battalion with 45 vehicles (of which 38 were delivered), which were to be available in time for the Ardennes (Battle of the Bulge) offensive.

At the beginning of 1945, it was decided to supply the Panzer IV/70(A) in only relatively small numbers to assault gun units. Due to the higher effective range of their weapon, they were also to provide tactical support for the assault guns/tank destroyers equipped with the 7.5cm StuK L/48.

On 1 March 1945, the commander of H StuGBrig 276 declared his unit no longer combat-capable. In a combat strength report, he described his unit as well staffed and equipped but only two assault guns – both in need of repair – were available.

On 22 March 1945, according to other sources, the unit was issued with three Panzer IV/70(A).

Unfortunately, only a few records regarding assault gun battalions have survived, therefore no field or after-action reports on the use of the Panzer IV/70(A) exist.

The overall height of the Alkett-designed Panzer IV/70 (A) was 35cm more than that on the VOMAG type. The final vehicles produced by Nibelungenwerk were fitted with wire mesh side skirts as used on the PzKpfw IV Ausf J.

Jagdpanther 5

From 1942, the German tank destroyer was developed in conjunction with the *Panzerwaffe* – both driven by the threat of superior enemy weapons.

After the completion of development work on the 7.5cm PaK 40 L/46, it was introduced as the standard weapon for the tank destroyer units. The same weapon was successfully installed in the PzKpfw IV and also the StuG.

Rheinmetall-Borsig had also developed a high-performance gun, the 7.5cm KwK 42 L/70, which was to be installed in the new PzKpfw V Panther medium tank. The aim was to achieve a clear performance advantage over the Russian armed forces. The use of this gun in the PzKpfw IV and StuG was ruled out for technical reasons. In order to give the troops a weapon that would guarantee them long-term superiority on the battlefield, the HWa now also demanded a leap into the next class – 8.8cm.

The troops had already been impressed at the effectiveness of this weapon during the invasion of France. In the rapid *Blitzkreig* operations, the 8.8cm FlaK L/56 heavy anti-aircraft gun was used to combat bunkers and heavy tanks. The *General der Artillerie* demanded the installation of this weapon in the assault gun, primarily to combat bunker systems. These plans were not feasible, but instead the 8.8cm FlaK L/56, appropriately modified, was mounted in the PzKpfw VI Ausf E Tiger in 1942.

The 8.8cm FlaK 18 and also 8.8cm FlaK 36 were further developed to match the increased altitudes of enemy aircraft. This new weapon, the 8.8cm FlaK 41 L/74, had a significantly longer barrel compared with earlier models, giving a muzzle velocity of more than 1,000mps. Due to this ballistic performance, it seemed to be fundamentally well suited for fighting tanks. At an armament meeting on 4 June 1942, Hitler demanded the immediate development of a tank destroyer weapon based on the FlaK 41. By September, key points

Opposite: A recovery crew from the Royal Tank Regiment examine an abandoned *Jagdpanther*. The 8.8cm PaK 43/3 L/71 had an exceptional ballistic performance that was superior to all enemy anti-tank guns and its thick, sloping frontal armour was virtually impenetrable. (Getty)

The *Panzerjäger-Schule*, formed in early 1944 at Mielau (Mlava), Poland, was responsible for training JgdPz units. This unarmed *Jagdpanther* was one of those specifically issued for driver training.

for the introduction of a motor-drawn weapon, the 8.8cm PaK 43/41 and a self-propelled gun (*Hornisse* [hornet], later renamed *Nashorn* [rhinoceros]) were decided. In spring 1943, this armament also became available for installation in the *Ferdinand* heavy assault gun.

An installation of this excellent weapon in the PzKpfw V Panther was technically (as of 1942) not possible, because the recoil was too long for the relatively small turret.

However, even before production of the PzKpfw V Panther began, it had also been decided to use the chassis to create an assault gun. A simple logic was followed here. According to German experience, a heavier weapon could be installed if a turret was dispensed with. Thus, a large casemate-type superstructure, with sloping 80mm front and 50mm side armour, was mounted on a *Panther* hull. Finally, the *General der Artillerie* was going to get what he wanted – an 8.8cm-armed StuG.

The 8.8cm PaK 43/3 L/71 was installed on space-saving mounting on the sloped front plate of the superstructure. Up to 57 rounds of 8.8cm ammunition could be carried internally.

Production of the new assault gun designated SdKfz 173, first called *Panzerjäger Panther* and subsequently *Jagdpanther*, initially began in January

1944 at Mühlenbau und Industrie Aktiengesellschaft (MIAG) in Braunschweig. Since the company could not produce the expected numbers for various reasons, two other companies were called in, Maschinenfabrik Niedersachsen Hannover (MNH) and Maschinenbau und Bahnbedarf (MBA) in Potsdam. A total of 413 units had left the production lines by April 1945.

As in the case of the *Ferdinand*, the vehicles were intended to be delivered to heavy tank destroyer detachments of 45 *Jagdpanther* each. Just like the StuGAbt of the assault artillery, the s PzJgAbt were available at army troop level and to be deployed in a targeted manner during focal point operations. The battalion officially consisted of three companies, each with 14 *Jagdpanther* (according to KStN 1149 'a'). The staff company had another three *Befehlsjäger* (command) version of the *Jagdpanther*, fitted with more powerful radio equipment.

However, the initial low output of *Jagdpanther* led to insufficient allocations and s PzJgAbt 654 was the only unit to receive the full complement of 45 *Jagdpanther* and three *Bergepanther* (recovery vehicle). The other battalions could only be re-equipped slowly and, in fact, never attained full strength. Subsequently, s PzJgAbt 519, PzJgAbt 559, PzJgAbt 560, PzJgAbt 563, PzJgAbt 616 and PzJgAbt 655 followed, all of which received only one company issued with the new vehicle (14 plus three *Befehlsjäger*). Those s PzJgAbt equipped with the *Jagdpanther* had considerable combat effectiveness, at least on paper, although in reality hardly any of these units reached the authorized target

Without the weight of a gun and mantlet, the *Jagdpanther* had a much higher ground clearance at the front. Next to it is the chassis of an assault gun fitted with a slave weight over the superstructure to simulate a heavier vehicle.

strength. Missing *Jagdpanther* had to be replaced by assault guns: 14 StuG III for each of the other two companies.

Furthermore, some *Heer* (army) and *Waffen*-SS units finally received small allocations, totalling some 150 vehicles.

A good example of the slow pace of deliveries is s PzJgAbt 654. On 1 July, the unit reported an inventory of 25 *Jagdpanther* at the tank training camp near the town of Mailly-le-Camp in north-eastern France. According to the report, field readiness had been reached, and the commander declared two companies ready for loading. The 1.Kp remained in the camp since the lack of tanks made training impossible. The commander sent another worrying message – just to make the existing *Jagdpanther* ready for combat, the initial supply of spare parts had been almost completely exhausted. Subsequently, both companies were

One of the two *Jagdpanther* 0-series produced in November 1943, undergoing trials. Initially, the 8.8cm PaK 43/3 L/71 was fitted with a one-piece barrel but, from May 1944, all guns were produced with a two-piece type.

soon in the field without stores of spare parts.

As late as August 1944, the 1.Kp still reported the absence of *Jagdpanther*. Even the vitally necessary SdKfz 9 heavy half-track tractors had not been delivered. It was not until early September that the battalion commander reported the arrival of 22 *Jagdpanther*. Nevertheless, serious problems remained. The unit was missing one armoured half-track vehicle, ten *Kübelwagen*, six motorcycles, nine heavy trucks, three *Maultier* (mule) half-track trucks, one SdKfz 10, one SdKfz 9 and also two SdKfz 9/1 *Drehkrankraftwagen* (crane-mounted vehicle), and consequently the operational readiness of the unit was seriously endangered. Due to the lack of three heavy tractors, the recovery of a damaged *Jagdpanther* was not guaranteed. Engine and gearbox repairs were almost impossible due to the lack of cranes. Even more concerning was the lack

The commander of an early production *Jagdpanther:* He wears a splinter pattern camouflage uniform with standard-issue *Doppel-Fernhöhrer* (earphones) and *Kehlkopf-Mikrofon* (throat-type microphone).

of essential parts including the required: seven Maybach HL 230 engines, five gearboxes, 23 sets of tracks and 23 drive sprockets.

This report by Major Hermann Sachtleben, the commander of s PzJgAbt 654, seems to be more of a call for help:

> The Panther-type final drive, even in its strengthened version, is completely unsuitable for the *Jagdpanther,* which is a very top-heavy vehicle. The drive units supplied lasted an average of 35km before failing. This is due to the stub axle on the two intermediate wheels being overstressed. It is imperative that these stub axles are redesigned. However, according to the chief designer at the factory, no significant improvement can be expected.

After only a few weeks in action, s PzJgAbt 654 was virtually non-operational. In September, it was only just possible to save the remaining serviceable *Jagdpanther* by moving them across the Seine. The Gen d PzTrp: West ordered immediate replenishment.

In the summer of 1944, Guderian stated at a Führer meeting that the initial mechanical problems with the PzKpfw V Panther had been completely resolved. But this cannot be said for the *Jagdpanther* issued to s PzJgAbt 654.

On 28 September 1944, s PzJgAbt 559 sent a field report to the office of the GenInsp d PzTrp. At that time, the unit had reported 18 *Jagdpanther* at its disposal, not two companies. To ensure combat readiness, the missing vehicles were replaced by an unknown number of StuG.

s PzJgAbt 559 [Panther]
28 September 1944

After-action report:

During the attacks on the bridgehead in Beeringen [Belgium], where strong tank forces were to be expected due to reconnaissance and infantry reports, only one StuG company was deployed in isolation due to the situation. Only in the course of the fighting, when it became clear that the assault guns could not prevail in every situation against the numerically superior enemy tanks, was the *Jagdpanther*-equipped company also deployed to the bridgehead. This piecemeal deployment resulted in us taking heavy losses. The battalion is convinced that a united offensive operation conducted by a mixed deployment of the StuG and *Jagdpanther* would have led to the destruction of all the enemy tanks involved. The bridgehead would have been cleared and our losses would have been considerably lower. In such an operation, the *Jagdpanther* would have destroyed the enemy tanks, the more agile StrG assault guns would have taken over the close-range and flank protection and, after destroying the enemy tanks, would have served to pull the infantry forward. Although the companies were attached to the regiments, the attack had to be led predominantly by the *Jagdpanther.* The reasons for this are as follows:

The ambush style of camouflage on this series production *Jagdpanther* was applied by the manufacturer prior to delivery. The gun has the two-piece barrel introduced on production vehicles in May 1944.

This 0-series *Jagdpanther* was also not given a coating of Zimmerit anti-magnetic paste. Originally fitted with two vision blocks, the *Fahroptik* (driver's optic) was removed while still in production and the opening plated over.

- Leading a *Jagdpanther* company on a wide front using radio communications is easier than leading infantry units.
- The infantry relies very closely on the armoured weapons and inevitably follows their every move.

Subsequently, our aim should be that, for all assault operations, the command of the entire attack is transferred to the leader of the armoured unit. If the infantry commander is given command of the entire attack, he must exert his influence on the tanks and his infantry by concise radio communications. However, the tactically correct use of the armoured forces must always remain the overriding principle.

In previous operations, it has always been very difficult to detach the armoured forces from an infantry formation and then deploy them to other identified centres of main effort. The infantry leaders' overriding and understandable concerns about security, wanting to keep the armoured forces to their rear at all costs, were given way too much consideration by the commander. As a result, the vehicles could not always be deployed tactically in the right place.

The *Jagdpanther* battalion efforts to assist the tanks out of the combat zone after a mission and hold them in reserve were ignored. As a result, the tanks remained in direct action until they either broke down completely or were so damaged that they had to be taken to the workshop for major repairs and were thus out of action for a long time.

As a result, the *Jagdpanther* company, which should have been serviced after 250km, had to travel over 600km without any maintenance. The detrimental effect this had on the vehicles, and thus on the combat strength of the division, is proven by numerous examples.

In summary, the [*Jagdpanther*] battalion's aims are as follows:

1.) Closed deployment of the battalion under the leadership of its commander.

2.) Close co-operation between infantry units deployed within the battalion.

3.) When *Jagdpanther* and infantry are deployed, the infantry must adapt to the fighting style of the tank destroyers, not vice versa. The entire operation must be structured according to these aspects.

4.) After each operation, all *Jagdpanther* must be immediately be disingaged and deployed as a mobile reserve behind the assigned combat sector.

The side armour on the hull of the *Jagdpanther* was, like that of many German tanks, vulnerable to anti-tank fire. Here, two shells have penetrated the engine bay and immobilized the vehicle. In the background is a knocked-out US Army M36 tank destroyer, one of the few Allied types that could threaten a *Jagdpanther* in front-on combat.

Although the two-piece gun barrel became available in May 1944, remaining stocks of the one-piece type continued to be used until October. The style in which the Zimmerit anti-magnetic paste coating has been applied indicates that the vehicle was manufactured by MIAG. Note the modified driver´s optic.

The office of the GenInsp d Pz Trp commented:

The battalion is striving for a united operation to be approved. The combined firepower that then comes into effect guarantees rapid and resounding success with low own losses. In addition, the leadership always has the entire combat power of the battalion at its disposal. If there are several focal points of attack at the same time over a wide area, and our armoured forces are limited, a united deployment of the battalion would not always be possible. The resulting deployment in company strength does not correspond to the nature of the tank destroyer battalion.

The mixed use of the *Jagdpanther* and StuG takes account of the structure of the battalion and brings an advantageous complement of great firepower, range and the substantial armour of the *Jagdpanther,* as well as by the small assault guns that easily disappear in the terrain.

The final assembly hall at the MNH factory, Hanover, where production began in April 1944. Due to the commonality of a number of components, it was possible to assemble the PzKpfw V Panther and *Jagdpanther* in parallel. Note the Maybach HL 230 TRM engines ready to be installed.

Cooperation with the infantry is above all a matter of constant training and the creation of a mutual understanding. This must be ensured through detailed discussions between the leaders of the infantry and the armoured unit before the battle, and the type of communication to be employed during the battle must be arranged (handing over of radios to the infantry).

Regarding the requirement of 'adapting' the infantry to the fighting style of the *Jagdpanther*, the following can be said:

With regard to the structure of the attack (deep or wide), the infantry must be guided by the armoured unit, as this depends on the local terrain. The speed of the attack is firstly determined by the speed of the *Jagdpanther* and secondly by the pace of the PzGren. The tank has to make full use of its mobility and speed for its individual movements and then to supervise the advance of the grenadiers from a skilfully chosen position. The decisive factor for success is that the connection between our armour and the grenadiers is not lost.

The thinking behind many infantry commanders' attempts to keep an individual tank as a back-up in their section is flawed. The *Jagdpanther* is not a positional anti-tank gun but a mobile weapon with which to attack focal points on the battlefront.

In the final stages of their training course at Mielau, prospective drivers received instruction on a fully equipped *Jagdpanther*. The pattern of the factory-applied Zimmerit anti-magnetic paste indicates that the vehicle was produced by MIAG.

Allied air superiority over the Normandy battlefront caused German forces to not only carefully camouflage their vehicles, but also to carry out any movements between dusk and dawn.

This mobility can only be maintained if engineers are given sufficient time and opportunity to carry out regular mechanical maintenance and repair. For this purpose, they must be pulled out of the frontline between missions.

It must have been clear to the GenInsp d PzTrp that the necessity of mixed-equipment *Jagdpanther* units did not follow the stringent operational doctrine, but was caused by the insufficient performance of German heavy industry. In the example described, there were simply too few of the powerful *Jagdpanther*; missing vehicles had to be substituted with other JgdPz or StuG. This resulted in many disadvantages for the units, and the supply of spare parts and maintenance became more complex and costly. The tactical principles also had to be adapted to this reality.

The GenInsp d PzTrp calls this an 'advantageous connection' between two different vehicles. In some respects, this assessment is incorrect or incomplete.

The broad attack of a unit fully equipped with *Jagdpanther* (45 vehicles), which was considered ideal according to tactical doctrine, was not possible for mixed units. This was not least because the number of operational JgdPz was often less than 50 percent of the established strength due to losses at the front and vehicles in need of repair.

In theory, the lighter assault guns or tank destroyers were supposed to provide flank cover for the attacking *Jagdpanther*. This meant that, in many situations, the superior weapon effect and front armour of the *Jagdpanther* could not be fully exploited, since the vehicles – armed with 7.5cm PaK L/48 – could not engage every enemy at long range. As soon as the attack came closer to enemy positions or tanks, these vehicles were much more exposed to offensive fire.

The officer invoked the service regulation applicable to his weapon, which required him to take the tactical lead when attached to an infantry unit, or at least to consistently present the limitations of his weapon. This led to time-consuming confrontations in many cases. The report also reveals that the German units, forced onto the defensive, had lost all initiative. The coordination between the combat troops lying in the trenches and the armoured units that were sent to support them was unsatisfactory. The lack of experienced, battle-hardened and mentally resilient leaders and soldiers was particularly noticeable on the Western Front. There, the Allied forces employed their air superiority with deadly effect, which further crushed the morale of the German soldiers.

There are many indications that the operational principles of the *Jagdpanther* were willfully or deliberately disregarded because of the tense situation at the front. The valuable vehicles were given tasks that were conceptually and, above

In September 1944, the heavily battered s PzAbt 654 was transferred back to its home garrison. In October, the replenished unit began training at Grafenwöhr with new support units, which included a *Panzer-Flugzeugabwehrkanone-Zug* (PzFlaKZg – armoured anti-aircraft platoon) with four 2cm FlaK 38 *Wirbelwind* (whirlwind) and four 3.7cm FlaK 43 *Möbelwagen* (furniture van).

Above: In 1943, *Panzerschürzen* began to be fitted as a standard item on all German Panzer, StuG and JgdPz to protect against fire from Red Army 14.5mm anti-tank rifles. The plates were also reasonably effective against shaped charge ammunition.

Right: October 1944: A *Jagdpanther* from s PzAbt 654 on the training grounds at Grafenwöhr after the unit had been re-equipped and was preparing to return to the frontline.

all, technically beyond their capabilities. If *Jagdpanther* commanders were not able to assert their force against the combat troops, such an inappropriate deployment quickly led to heavy losses and the objective could not be achieved.

It was often not understood that, while the PzGren at the front needed the help of the *Jagdpanther*, these turretless vehicles were themselves absolutely dependent on *Begleit-Grenadiere* (escort grenadiers) who stayed near the tanks to protect them against enemy anti-tank close-combat teams.

In 1944, s PzJgAbt 519 had been decimated in the turmoil of *Operatsiya* (Operation) *Bagration*, during which all their *Nashorn* self-propelled tank destroyers were lost. The surviving personnel of the battalion were instructed to report for re-equipment at Mielau on 22 August 1944.

The battalion was to be exclusively equipped with *Jagdpanther*, but this was not possible due to the production situation. Consequently, only one company with 14 *Jagdpanther* could be assigned to this unit; the second and third companies were issued with 14 StuG III each. The division staff had another three command *Jagdpanther*.

In October, the unit was deployed on the Western Front. The number of operational vehicles decreased as the time of deployment lengthened. On 1 December 1944, four out of the 17 *Jagdpanther* and six out of the 28 StuG were reported as being operational.

On 7 January 1945, the unit reported an actual inventory (operational and in repair) of eight *Jagdpanther*, 19 StuG III and eight Pz IV/70(V). The latter probably reached the unit as replacements. Although they possessed excellent firepower, the presence of vehicles built on PzKpfw IV chassis further exacerbated the maintenance situation and the already precarious supply of spare parts.

On 1 March 1945, the commander of s PzJgAbt 519 delivered a report:

> 1.) Training level:
> Satisfactory. Replacements that have arrived require further education and training. The driver replacements, especially for PzKpfw (*), are completely unsuitable for use on this front.
> 2.) Morale of the troop:
> Satisfactory.
> 3.) Special difficulties:
> In the last period, the battalion was transferred several times to different combat areas and sometimes thrown into battle in a hurry. Due to the fuel shortage and the dispersion of the recovery group and workshop over an area of 80km, the division suffered losses of armoured fighting vehicles that were absolutely avoidable. The replacement of failed PzKpfw (*) is extremely difficult at the moment. The general

The commander of this *Jagdpanther* has positioned his vehicle under the cover of trees at the edge of a forest to prevent being spotted by marauding Allied ground-attack aircraft. The vehicle is in service with s PzJgAbt 654 and carries the tactical number 234.

shortage of spare parts, especially for the PzKpfw IV (**), is making itself strongly felt in the maintenance section.

(*) This refers to armoured vehicles such as JgdPz and StuG.
(**) PzKpfw IV-based *Flakpanzer* (anti-aircraft tank).

Towards the end of the war, and when the tactical situation permitted, remarkable successes were still achievable.

In March 1945, s PzJgAbt 653 was engaged in heavy fighting around East Prussia. The 1.Kp was equipped with nine *Jagdpanther*, the 2.Kp and 3.Kp were issued with 12 Pz IV/70 each. After only a short briefing and training on the new equipment, the vehicles attacked north of Allenstein. A press report, certainly coloured by propaganda, describes the fighting in dramatic language:

> The spoils of a single Panther (*): 33 tanks knocked out in three days. *Oberfeldwebel* Bleyer receives the Knight's Cross as a PzKpfw V Panther commander.

> 24 March 1945. The enemy races over the positions of the *Niedersachsen-Division* [Lower Saxony Division] in a barrage. Artillery, automatic guns, mortars and anti-tank guns pound the acres of fields. With submachine guns, the commissars force the Soviet assault battalions into battle behind the T-34s. The sky over East Prussia is grey. The Panthers wait in hollows and along wooded areas with their crews feverish with impatience. Wherever their paws reach, the earth shakes, the steel skeletons of the Soviet tanks break like glass. Five tanks are counted on the first day. Six tanks fall on the second day, and a heavy anti-tank

gun is also killed. On this day, Bleyer's tank is on the right flank of the division. On the left, the battle rages like a witch's cauldron. Bleyer pulls the Panther behind the front into the middle of the crashing impacts. This day belongs to the Panthers of his heavy PzJgAbt and the Lower Saxons. Soon 22 enemy tanks are left burning. Bled dry, the Bolshevik guards go back to their woods and wait to be relieved.

The following morning, two Panther commanders go out to assess the effect of their hits. They see five – six – seven enemy tanks ready to fight in a hollow. They themselves are a good 1,000m away from their tanks. Here they gather and hold a quiet conversation, and soon they are back. The Panthers drive off, and soon the gunners spot the pack of tanks. At 1,400m there are eight tanks, three of them standing close together. The guns roar, tanks burn over there, smoke rises. At the end, seven torches shine in the fields.

Today the major hung the Knight's Cross around Bieyer's neck. The photographer captured the smiling face of Bieyer with the medal. Until the day before yesterday, he had destroyed a total of 48 tanks, a good record in East Prussia.

Kriegsberichter [war correspondent] Karl Otto Zottmann

(*) These are the *Jagdpanther* of s PzJgAbt 653.

In terms of its weapons, performance and excellent level of protection, the *Jagdpanther* theoretically had a high combat effectiveness. Used responsibly and with tactical skill – i.e. awareness of their strengths and weaknesses – the vehicles, which were almost invulnerable to front-on attack at long ranges, could achieve great success.

The biggest problem, however, was the chronic unreliability of the drive components. If the heavy *Jagdpanther*, like the StuG, remained in service for too long, the need for thorough maintenance increased. If this could not be ensured, the danger grew that the vehicles would be immobilized due to even minor damage. Salvage was often impossible in the heat of battle or due to insufficient recovery vehicles, leaving the crew to destroy a valuable vehicle to prevent it from falling into enemy hands. In fact, more *Jagdpanther* were probably lost through being blown up by their own forces than through enemy action.

The spare parts situation was to worsen towards the end of the war.

On 24 March 1945, s PzJgAbt 654 reported:

Urgently need three complete 8.8cm KwK 43/3. Where can collection by the battalion take place?

On 11 April 1945, *Oberleutnant* Bock, an officer in the field bureau of the

Battle of the Bulge: German field engineers were attempting to replace the right final drive assembly on this *Jagdpanther,* but had to abandon their task to avoid being captured by US troops. An 8.8cm SprGr has been left in front of the hull.

GenInsp d PzTrp, sent an alarming report:

Travel report for the period 8 to 10 April 1945

I had the task of obtaining status reports from the PzDiv of the 6.Army and the 8.Army and to establish why an unusually large number of JgdPz were blown up by *schwere Heeres-Panzerjäger-Abteilung* (s H PzJgAbt – heavy tank destroyer battalion at army level) 560 during the retreat movements in Hungary. Consultation with the commander of battalion, at the time attached to 12.SS-PzDiv Hitlerjugend, regarding the extremely large number of fighting tanks blown up during the withdrawal of units along the German border with Hungary revealed the following:

The battalion was attached to the 12.SS-PzDiv HJ and deployed as the 3.Abt of the PzRgt. The supply company of the battalion was combined with the parts supply section of the PzRgt to form a so-called *Versorgungsgruppe* (supply group). The recovery services of the battalion were also taken over by the regiment in order to centrally control salvage and repair. This deprived the commander of any influence on supply and maintenance. Moreover, since his orderly officer had to be seconded to the regiment, there was no man available to take care of these matters within s H PzJgAbt 560.

During the retreat from Bakony forest to Ödenburg, the battalion was not allocated any fuel at all. Consequently, only nine PzJg IV and three *Jagdpanther* could be salvaged, by recklessly taking fuel from other units.

Most incidents of tanks being blown up by crews were due to a lack of organization in the recovery service, which was supposed to be carried out centrally by the regiment. The latter preferred to use their own vehicles; the recovery of the *Jagdpanther* of sH PzJgAbt 560 was always postponed until the very end. In most cases it was then already too late to carry out a recovery. The locations of many *Jagdpanther* – which had often become bogged down or suffered some minor mechanical damage – had been overrun and occupied by Red Army infantry. For example, the first attempt to recover a *Jagdpanther,* which had become bogged down on 8 March 1945, did not take place until 21 March.

Constant requests and urgent pleas from the battalion commander for the allocation of recovery resources to the regiment and the division remained fruitless in the vast majority of cases. It was often remarked that there were no means of salvage available and that, in an emergency, the vehicle should be blown up.

The PzRgt had complete control of the JgdPz. Repaired vehicles of the battalion were assigned to any unit without informing the battalion. Thus the commander was never aware of how many operational fighting vehicles were available or even where they were located.

Another reason for the many losses of JgdPz was their tactically incorrect deployment. Almost without exception, they were deployed in the manner of assault guns. In some cases, they were left behind together with infantry forces

A bomb dropped by an Allied ground-attack aircraft has blown this *Jagdpanther* off the road and on to its roof. The force of the explosion has opened a gap where the floor plate joins the bow plate. Any surviving crewmen would have escaped through the large hatch in the rear of the superstructure. (NARA)

Men from the Royal Tank Regiment use a *Jagdpanther* to recover another from a French town. Both were abandoned by s PzJgAbt 654 during the battle for Normandy in 1944.

as a rearguard against the enemy. This is extremely unfavourable for vehicles that can only fire to the front, as they have to turn around every time they move into position. In some situations, damaged *Jagdpanther* were ordered to be dug-in, an impossible mission for vehicles with purely forward-firing weapons. The result was the loss of these vehicles, which had to be blown up to prevent them from falling into enemy hands.

Due to the fact that the PzRgt was completely in charge of the tactical operations, as well as of supply, recovery and repair, a responsible leadership of the s PzJgAbt 560 by its own commander was not possible. He was practically only a company commander of the tank regiment.

Multi-loading

At the end of the war, US Army officers searching Kummersdorf found the prototype of a multi-loading device intended for use in the *Jagdpanther*. This 'cartridge drum' was fitted behind the gun mounting and could hold six shells. The frame and ammunition-carrying drum rotated around a horizontal axle for cartridges to feed into the breech. Both operations were done manually.

Festungs-PaK (Anti-Fortress Gun)

In 1944, there was apparently a large surplus of 8.8cm PaK 43/3 L/71 guns in *Jagdpanther* mounts; far more than were needed for installation in JgdPz. On 24 September 1944, during an armament meeting with Hitler, it was decided:

> The Führer considers the proposed makeshift pedestal gun carriage for the installation of the surplus *Jagdpanther* 8.8cm KwK 43/3 guns for site-specific use to be very essential. The ordered 400 pedestal gun mounts are to be delivered, as proposed, starting with 40 pieces arriving, at the latest, in the first days of October, followed by at least 40 pieces every week thereafter. The details are to be fixed with the HWa and the commander of the pioneers.

The guns were installed in fixed field positions on all fronts. Such a use of these valuable weapons hardly made sense under the conditions of the mobile war, which the Germans had employed for the first time in 1939 and the Allied forces successfully copied. After reconnaissance, the positions became easy targets for enemy fighter-bombers and artillery.

Towards the end of the war, a rotating loading device, holding six shells, was designed for the *Jagdpanther*. The item was intended to ease the workload of the *Laderschütz* (loader) and would certainly have increased the rate of fire. When the war ended, any intact devices were sent to the US for examination and evaluation.

Jagdpanzer 38 6

The devastating bombing raids on the Alkett factory in Berlin-Borsigwalde on 23 November and 26 November 1943 caused the production of the important StuG to collapse. While 257 vehicles left the assembly lines in October, only 98 did so in November. Since it no one could forecast when the October figure could be reached again, the HWa reacted and decided to produce the assault gun on the chassis of the PzKpfw IV.

BMM in Prague was also contacted. The company had continuously supplied the *Wehrmacht* with the PzKpfw 38(t) light tank until March 1942. After that, the hull was used for the development for various types of tank destroyer and self-propelled artillery. All these vehicles performed well within their capabilities. However, BMM was not in a position to take up production of the assault gun, as the lifting equipment at the factory only allowed it to handle loads of up to some 15,000kg. Due to the urgency of the situation, it was decided in December 1943 to develop a new, light self-propelled assault gun using components from the PzKpfw 38(t).

Within a very short time the planning was completed and, by March, three prototypes were ready for trials.

The standard hull was slightly widened and fitted with a *Kasematte* (casemate)-type superstructure fabricated from sloping armour plates. The 60mm front armour provided good protection, but the 20mm side armour was only safe against fire from 7.92mm armour-piercing ammunition. Close-range fire from 14.5mm PTR and 14.5mm PTRD anti-tank rifles, in service with the Red Army, remained dangerous.

As in the StuG, the 7.5cm PaK 39 L/48 was installed in a mounting fitted on the sloping front plate. A total of 41 shells were carried in the fighting compartment, leaving little space for the four-man crew.

Opposite: A *Jagdpanzer* 38 abandoned during the defence of Prague in 1945. The turretless vehicle was unsuited to street fighting and any such deployment would need to be supported by infantry. The type became known to troops in the field as the *Hetzer*, which was probably derived from the term *Hetzjagd* (wild hunt).

On 20 April 1944, the first 20 JgdPz 38 completed were presented to Adolf Hitler on the occasion of his birthday. Some vehicles were still incomplete – for example, the heavy cast mantlet is missing.

An innovative weapon for self-defence was installed in front of the gunner's hatch. The 7.92mm *Rundumfeuer-Maschinengewehr* (all-round fire machine gun) 34 could be guided remotely from the interior and allowed the crew to engage enemy infantry at close range.

However, there were certain limits to the tactical deployment of the vehicle. The relatively weak side armour, should have been even thicker than that used on the StuG or PzJgiIV. The lateral traverse of the gun was only six degrees to the left, necessitating constant steering of the vehicle at the expense of mechanical components such as the final drive units.

Moreover, the original specification could not be fully met. The specified combat weight of 13,000kg was exceeded by 3,000kg, which meant the Praga Wilson transmission was operating at the limit. Although engine power was increased from 125hp in the PzKpfw 38(t) to 150hp, the power-to-weight ratio dropped from 12.7hpt to 9.4hpt. Also, the required top speed of 60kph was not achieved.

Initially the vehicle was designated *leichter Panzerjäger* 38, abbreviated to le PzJg 38, but from October 1944 this was changed to *Jagdpanzer* 38 (JgdPz 38). When assigned to independent PzJgAbt (45 JgdPz 38) and other units of the *Panzertruppe*, the standard radio equipment consisted of a Fu 5 transmitter and receiver with 2m *Stabsantenne* (rod antenna). Command vehicles (two at division level and one at company level) were fitted with an additional Fu 8 radio with a long-range transmitter. This required an extra *Sternantenne* (star antenna) 'd', which was mounted on the left side of the superstructure with an armoured box protecting the porcelain insulator.

Those that were assigned to infantry divisions most probably had a single FuSprech 'f' transceiver, whereas command vehicles probably had a more powerful device.

On the occasion of his birthday on 20 April 1944, the first 20 production *Jagdpanzer* 38 were displayed to Adolf Hitler on the *Reichautobahn* (state motorway) near Dresden. A short time later, the *General der Artillerie*, who was also counting on allocations for the assault artillery, noted in his war diary:

Twenty JzJg38 were lined up on the *Reichsautobahn* (state highway), with the limousines of Hitler and his entourage parked on the opposite carriageway. All the tank destroyers are painted *Dunkelgelb* (dark yellow), but the guns are bare steel.

The PzJg 38

The first deliveries still have development defects and are not yet battlefield-ready. Delivery to the field army will begin around mid-June.

As late as June 1944, the general staff of the army stated:

Of the 170 StuG 38(t) (*) to be delivered by 1 July 1944 according to the *Rüstungsheft* (armament records), only 36 had been delivered to the army by 20 June: 14 to the reserve army, seven to the *Panzerjäger-Schule*, Mielau, and 15 to Kummersdorf, Putlos, and other establishments for testing and trials.

The first 20 assault guns presented to the Führer on 20 April were immediately returned to the factory after the event because they were not yet operational. Among other items, even parts of their armour were not installed.

After this was remedied, it was found that the vehicle weighed 15,000kg and not the projected 13,000kg. This resulted in an overstressed transmission.

A tank destroyer unit on the training grounds at Mielau. The *Sternantenne* (star antenna) 'd', for additional Fu 8 radio equipment, indicates that this JgdPz 38 is in service as a *Befehlsjäger.*

Modifications: The armour is to be changed at the rear to balance the weight. Furthermore, a new gearbox is currently being developed. In order to remedy the top-heaviness, which has negatively changed the driving characteristics, the front suspension must be strengthened.

Result: The StuG 38(t) is still at the development and testing stage.

(*) In 1944, the designations *Sturmgeschütz*, *Panzerjäger* and *Jagdpanzer* were synonymous. Officially, the designation JgdPz 38 was adopted for the type.

The development of the new tank destroyer took place within a very short time, with only four months between the first draft and the delivery of the prototype. Once again it became apparent that achieving wartime usability could not be guaranteed in such a short time. Before the war, the HWa considered a time frame of between 18 and 24 months as being necessary for comparable projects. This allowed intensive testing of the pre-production vehicles, so that the experience gained could be evaluated and any necessary modifications implemented.

Many of the JgdPz 38 produced by BMM left the factory already painted in *Licht-und-Schatten Tarnung*. The vehicle is fitted with the lighter type of cast mantlet and the rotatable machine-gun mounting.

BMM was able gradually to eliminate the problems and increasing numbers of vehicles began rolling off the production line in June. After Škoda began assembling the type in July, up to 400 vehicles left the assembly halls every month. From August 1944, 230kg was saved by redesigning the gun mantlet and, in September, strengthened front leaf springs were installed.

By the end of the war, joint production of the JgdPz 38, by BMM and Škoda, had reached 2,800 vehicles.

Allocations

Initially, it was planned to issue the new tank destroyer in company strength to the infantry divisions as a highly mobile anti-tank weapon. The individual companies were to be equipped according to the standardized KStN 1149. In the February 1944 edition, this had either 10 or 14 vehicles (StuG III, PzJg IV or, depending on availability, JgdPz 38). A complement of 14 vehicles seems to have been the normal number assigned to the infantry, tank destroyer and cavalry divisions and also the *Volksgrenadier* (VGrenDiv).

For unknown reasons, however, the first units were to be raised as *selbständige Panzerjäger-Abteilungen* (slbs PzJgAbt – independent tank destroyer battalions), each with three companies. In July, PzJgAbt 731 was issued with 49 of the type and PzJgAbt 743 received 45. During September, a further 45 were

issued to PzJgAbt 741. These units were to be deployed at army troop level. In September 1944, PzJgAbt 561 was similarly equipped and, in February 1945, PzJgAbt 744 was formed.

However, the largest numbers of vehicles were issued to InfDiv, VGrenDiv and also SS units in company strength (the majority were issued with 14 vehicles, but some received only ten).

Later in the year, a new table, KStN 1149, was published in which the number of PzJg was reduced to 13, with one command vehicle being omitted.

On 10 August 1944, the Inspector General of the Army presented the first combat experiences with the JgdPz 38 to the Führer:

The standard-fit Fu 5 radio was positioned on the right-hand side of the fighting compartment, next to the commander. The 2m *Stabsantenne* (rod aerial) was mounted adjacent to it on the outside of the superstructure.

Operational experience with le PzJg 38 as of 1 August 1944

Tactical: Strong weapon effect with small size and favourable shape, good command possibilities by radio. Well suited and already proven for anti-tank operations, as well as for direct support of infantry attacks. One company knocked out 20 Red Army tanks within a short time. Front armour withstands fire from Russian 7.62cm anti-tank gun (*). But at the moment, the type is too slow for use within fully motorized formations.

Mechanical: Crews have confidence in the vehicle – despite it having a number of minor problems – because, when driven carefully, it remains without mechanical damage over longer distances. A more powerful engine would be desirable, as the JgdPz 38 is too slow off-road. Reverse gear should have a higher reduction ratio, as there is a risk of stalling.

(*) This statement seems unconvincing because it is too general.

In October, further experience and instructions on the deployment of the type were published in the *Nachrichtenblatt der Panzertruppe* (Bulletin of the Armoured Forces):

The JgdPz 38

The experiences of the first combat missions of the PgdPz 38 led to the following conclusions. These points have arisen during deployment and training:

Each tank destroyer division equipped with ten to 14 JgdPz 38 was issued with a *Bergepanzer* 38. The vehicle carried the components of an auxiliary crane that had the capacity to lift an engine or a 7.5cm PaK 39.

1.) The JgdPz 38 has passed its acid test. The crews are proud of their vehicles; they, as well as the infantry, have confidence in the type. The all-round fire MG is singled out for special praise. The low overall height of the vehicle and specific design have proven its full suitability for its main tasks, the fight against enemy tanks and the immediate support of the infantry in attack and defence. For example, a single company knocked out 20 tanks in a short time without any total failures. One battalion destroyed 57 tanks – including two *Josef Stalin* at 800m range – and did not suffer any losses to enemy guns during these tank battles. The division then arrived at their destination after a day's march of 160km without any mechanical failures.

2.) The smallest combat unit must be the platoon (four *Jäger*), only then is an effective concentration of fire and mutual support and surveillance possible. The united deployment of these units (*) has also always proved to be the most rational. It led most safely and quickly to a decisive success and thus ensured that the full combat power of the unit could be quickly freed up for other tasks. Also, time was gained for mechanical maintenance and repair.

3.) Any use below platoon strength is only justified in emergencies or under special terrain conditions. For these cases, the half platoon must be trained to fight as such and the leader must be capable of independent action (**).

4.) Tank destroyers must not be deployed alone. Especially for attack missions of all kinds on enemy positions. Here, grenadiers must always be assigned for immediate support and close protection.

5.) Every mission must be carefully thought through. A battle plan must be

From January 1945, the *Bergepanzer* (armoured recovery vehicle) 38 was equipped with a 5,000kg-capacity winch, as well as a rear-mounted recovery spade. On the right-hand side of the superstructure are the components of the lifting gear and towing gear. But, in service, the type proved to be too light to be effective.

A JgdPz 38 during winter trials on the snow fields around the Großglockner mountain in southern Austria. The vehicle is fitted with track extensions and a rudimentary snow plough, which was used to push snow under the tracks to increase ground clearance.

determined through detailed discussion between the leaders involved to clarify the distribution of tasks, the coordination of the weapons and the type of communication to be used during the battle.

6.) The platoon leader is always with his *Jäger*. The battalion commander is with the main force; he will command any attack above platoon strength. The battalion's command post must be located where communication links ensure a reliable connection to the grenadier regiments and to the division.

7.) When marching during the day, break up and disperse as much as possible and keep distances of 100m or more between the vehicles. Be alert to the constant danger of enemy air raids. Marching at night with the current driver's optics is only possible at a very slow pace by clear orders of the *Jäger* commander or by

sending a man ahead of each *Jäger*. Improved vision devices for the driver have been requested and will be implemented (***).

8.) Outside of combat, staging areas should be entered or left during twilight or darkness; preferably covered by the sound of an artillery barrage. Towns, as well as areas near road junctions (road crossings, bridges and railway facilities), are to be avoided.

9.) On the march and at the ready: Covering the vehicle with foliage has proved to be the best camouflage, but it must blend in with the surroundings. However, the crew must be able to remove it in a few seconds so that observation and firing are unhindered.

10.) Time must be allocated for mechanical maintenance and repair. After marches and between missions, there must be an opportunity for this work. Otherwise, defective vehicles will line the roads instead of being the decisive weapon.

11.) In combat against tanks and PaK, a low profile allows hunter-like stalking. The JgdPz 38 can, if spotted by the enemy, be quickly driven to another position and re-engage the enemy at effective range with concentrated fire. The front armour

Spring 1945: A JgdPz 38 carries a number of PzGren, many of whom appear to be armed with a 7.92mm *Sturmgewehr* (StG – assault rifle) 44, during the retreat back from the Soviet Union to defend the *Vaterlandlinie* (Fatherland Line).

The crew of this JgdPz 38 has decorated the mantlet with eyes and teeth. Such decoration had been previously used by the crews of assault guns.

withstands fire from Russian 7.62cm anti-tank guns. Failures have so far occurred only from hits on the side and rear armour. It is therefore particularly important to always show the enemy only its 'strong chest' [front armour]. Any movements across the front must be carried out outside of range of enemy fire.

12.) To repel attacking tanks or even massed infantry, the JgdPz 38 are to be kept ready in at least platoon strength, but outside the enemy's pre-attack barrage.

13.) In supporting a resolute counterattack, the JgdPz 38 has on several occasions contributed decisively to rapidly clearing enemy infantry from positions gained – it must never be used alone. The infantry must be informed before an attack that the tank destroyers often have to be driven back to replenish ammunition during the battle.

14.) The connection to the grenadiers was maintained during the battle by shouting messages. Target assignments for the grenadiers would be made by point shooting with the flare gun and shouting to the commander.

15.) The JgdPz 38 is not suitable for supporting attacks along tracks leading through marshy terrain. The vehicle gets bogged down when leaving the road. On the road, however, it is defenceless against enemy anti-tank guns that are concealed in the terrain and aware of its weak side armour.

16.) Use of the tank hunter within a motorized formation or battle group (armed reconnaissance) is not recommended, since the JgdPz 38 is too slow and vulnerable (****).

17.) In urban warfare (Warsaw), the JgdPz 38 proved itself ably due its maneuverability on the road. Here, the all-round fire MG was used to great advantage. However, since the gunner has to open the hatch to reload, defensive fire from another vehicle is necessary (prior communication by radio). In street fighting, the particularly close cooperation between the *Jäger* (*****), as well as with grenadiers and sappers, proved to be indispensable.

18.) Therefore, during training, radio communication, the use of the all-round fire MG and cooperation with the grenadiers must be continuously practised.

(*) *Panzerjäger* battalion with 45 of the type.
(**) This is the basis of the German *Auftragstaktik*.
(***) This change could not be introduced.
(****) It is interesting that 40kph was not considered sufficient.
(*****) The term *Jäger* (hunter) was used for all types of tank destroyer.

A JgdPz 38 lies abandoned, along with a number of vehicles, as German forces retreat back to the borders of the Fatherland. The vehicle has *Licht-und-Schatten* camouflage, which was specifically created for operating in the dense foliage and woodland of central Europe. Note the staggered black rectangles painted under the driver's vision slot, which were intended to confuse enemy gunners.

In July 1944, four weeks after the Normandy landings, 708.InfDiv was deployed to cut Allied supply lines. This operation failed and the unit joined the rapid withdrawal from France until it was trapped and almost annihilated near Le Mans. The few survivors were sent to Czechoslovakia, where 573.VGrenDiv was in the process of being formed; but, on 4 September 1944,

A *Marder* III Ausf M follows a company of well-camouflaged JgdPz 38 on one of the few paved roads in the area around Lake Balaton, Hungary. The first soldier is armed with a 5cm *Granatwerfer* (GrWrf – mortar) 36, although this weapon had been declared obsolete in 1943.

the division was redesignated 708.VGrenDiv. In October, PzJgStuGKp 1708 was issued with 14 JgdPz 38 and integrated into the division, which in turn was ordered to the Alsace region of France.

The majority of the personnel were inexperienced, as were the men of PzJgStuGKp 1708. Consequently, the company was not sufficiently trained, which made its combat effectiveness correspondingly low.

On 3 December 1944, the XXXXV.Army Corps sent a report to the *General der Panzer Truppen West* (GendPzTrp: West – general of armoured forces: West):

Oberleutnant Günther, commander of PzJgStuGAbt 1708 (3./PzJgAbt 708 in the 708.VGrenDiv) (*) reported today:

The company now attached to the 708.VGrenDiv was transported by rail and

Jagdpanzer 38   175

disembarked at Rothe (south of Schirmeck) early on 13 November. The company had been retrained to operate the JgdPz 38 instead of the towed 8.8cm PaK, and had 24 of the type and an escort platoon (one officer, four NCOs and 55 men), all equipped with the MP 43. Günther reported to the division while the company unloaded. On the evening of 13 November, the company received deployment orders and, despite the commander's protestations, the *Eins*-a [1a – field unit operations officer] of the division ordered the immediate deployment. His decision was made without prior reconnaissance – or any terrain orientation – and without well-practised cooperation with the grenadiers. For the attack, the unit was attached to the commander of an infantry battalion (a very weak battalion made up of dispersed, convalescing and low-morale troops). The planned attack on 14 November could not be launched because the promised infantry reinforcements did not arrive on time. At 13:30hrs, the US Army attacked with superior forces and could just be halted by the intervention of JgdPz 38. The company commander's request to withdraw the *Jäger* for a few kilometers during the night of 14–15 November for ammunition, refuelling and mechanical inspection was not granted. The assault guns were to take over the local defence at night and only very weak infantry forces were available for the security.

On 15 November, at 07:00hrs, the attack was to take place again, with an assault battalion on the left for support. Once again, this support did not arrive in time, and the attack did not take place at first. At 09:15hrs, the US forces attacked after once

Due to it being relatively small, simply constructed and light (16,000kg), the JgdPz 38 was easy for the field engineers to repair and maintain. The *Balkenkreuz* (cross made of two heavy baulks of timber) marking in solid black is an interesting detail.

During the turmoil of the last days of the war, many vehicles were lost due to the action by Czechoslovak partisans. Here, local citizens inspect an immobilized JgdPz 38 on which both tracks have been destroyed.

again 'blinding' our front-line positions with a smoke screen.

When the fog lifted, the Americans faced the assault guns at 40m to 50m range, especially on the left flank of the company. The *Jäger* immediately took up the fire fight. Two of our tank destroyers were quickly knocked out by enemy close-combat teams after the optics were damaged and two commanders were killed. At the same time, some six Shermans, covered with foliage and followed by infantry, attacked from the left flank. Shortly afterwards, eight Shermans advanced head-on against the company. Another JgdPz 38 was destroyed by enemy close-range fire. A platoon leader's vehicle became bogged down and had to be blown up. The enemy attacked from the right flank, and advanced shortly afterwards with infantry and anti-tank weapons. The battalion commander ordered the troops to be dropped in a wooded area to the rear and immediately became involved in a fierce firefight. Since another JgdPz remained bogged down, the PzJgKp could not follow immediately.

Then our infantry tried to repel the advance of the enemy infantry but suffered heavy losses. After the bogged-down tank had been recovered, the entire company retreated deeper into the forest. At this point, the enemy had already come within 70m to 80m. The PzJgKp only had the remnants of its escort platoon for support. Turning to the right was out of the question, since there was a German minefield. To the company's rear was a water obstacle that could not be crossed by the JgdPz.

The company commander decided to break through to the left towards a nearby village. Shortly after emerging from the forest, two of the JgdPz received direct hits and the company commander's vehicle was hit in the drive sprocket. The three vehicles burned immediately. The last two remaining *Jäger* also received direct hits from the flank shortly afterwards. The company lost two officers and ten men, and another three officers are considered missing. Seven men have been wounded, including two officers. The infantry convoy lost 30 men and nine JgdPz 38 had to be written off as a total loss.

The commander of JgdPzAbt 1708 had taken part in the fight. A court martial is to be instituted against the commander.

Current inventory of PzJgKp 1708: Five JgdPz 38 in long-term repair (two gearboxes, one final drive, two oil coolers). Due to the lack of spare parts, contact was made with PzJgRgt 11, which has 25 well-trained men in repair squads and good mechanical equipment and tools, as well as a *Bergepanzer* 38 recovery tank. The wheeled vehicles are in good condition. One *Maultier* is missing. The infantry convoy still has one officer, two NCOs and 24 men. The company still has nine full crews.

Signed: *Oberst* Ludwig Schanze

Local civilian engineers appear to have repaired the tracks, although two track pins remain protruding. Note the wood-fired gas generator mounted on a truck parked behind the JgdPz 38.

The Gen d PzTrp West, Horst Stumpff, commented on this report:

Statement from the GendPzTrp West on the report by *Generalleitnant* Schanze on the PzJg (StuG) Kp 1708:

This is the second case within two weeks that a PzJg (StuG) company was completely destroyed within a few days. The extent to which the company's inadequate training, due to the short time available and the lack of fuel, was to blame cannot, as yet, be determined from here. In any case, the tactical leaders are partly to blame, as they ordered the operation without taking into account

These JgdPz 38 were abandoned by a German unit in the spring of 1945, most probably due to a lack of fuel. The German supply structure collapsed in the final stages of the war as the lines of defence constantly moved.

the characteristics of the weapon and without considering the suggestions or justified objections by the commander of the PzJgAbt or the company commander. Attachment to an infantry battalion could, from the outset, result in becoming involved in many impracticable, isolated and dangerous operations. Cooperation with an infantry unit is, however, always preferable.

Such a deployment as that used for local defence during the night of 14–15 November must be rejected in the strongest possible terms. Because of the small traverse of the gun, the engine has to be running for the tank to be ready for action. Particularly in a newly formed unit with new equipment, special care must be taken to ensure sufficient mechanical maintenance. Small omissions can lead to serious

damage. For the operation on 15 November, the PzJgKp was deployed too far forward. If the enemy had launched his attack with an artillery assault as usual, it is likely that losses of JgdPz 38 would have been recorded from the beginning of the attack. Had the company been deployed in the depth of the main battlefield, it would, in all probability, have been able to hold its own successfully against the 14 enemy tanks reported. During the retreat movements, the JgdPz 38 is defenceless against enemy tanks and anti-tank guns. Therefore, it requires special fire support – a staggered withdrawal of individual tank destroyer platoons, fire protection by heavy weapons and anti-tank protection by the infantry.

The PzJgKp is the most effective weapon against enemy tanks available to a division commander. At the same time, in close cooperation with infantry escorts, it is the best weapon for counterattack. The prerequisites for successful deployment are as follows:

Two JgdPz 38 in the delivery yard at the BMM factory in Prague. Both are painted in a very elaborate *Hinterhaltt* (ambush) camouflage scheme.

- Use in favourable terrain.
- Time must be allowed for sufficient terrain reconnaissance.
- Sufficient time must be allowed for careful mechanical maintenance.

In order to prevent further such wastage of difficult-to-replace material in the future, it is considered necessary to hold the leaders in charge of this mission accountable.

Signed: *Generalleutnant* Horst Stumpff

This report shows the high dynamics that characterized the fighting in the West. The attacking US Army units mercilessly exploited every weakness of the defenders. Two German counterattacks could not take place due to a

Size comparison: A JgdPz 38 is dwarfed by a PzKpfw V Panther in service with 23.PzDiv. The heavy gun mantlet identifies it as an early production vehicle.

lack of coordination. The enemy recognized this momentary weakness and attacked in turn. Although assault guns had been in service for a long time, the limitations of turretless vehicles were not sufficiently considered. In addition, the JgdPz 38 were surprised at point-blank range, and the tactical leader was then overwhelmed. An orderly retreat was not achieved and, due to a lack of close reconnaissance, a total of nine JgdPz 38 were lost, a disastrous failure.

Officers, non-commissioned officers and crews of many tank and tank destroyer units deployed in the West showed great deficiencies in their training and combat experience due to their often hasty deployment. The situation in the East was different; what had grown there in combat experience over the years could not be reproduced at will in the new deployments after the Normandy landings.

As reported on the occasion of a lecture to the Führer in December 1944, the troops used a suggestive name instead of the official designation JgdPz 38:

Explanation of the name *Hetzer:*

The term *HetzJagd* [wild hunt] has been adapted to *Hetzer* by our front-line troops when referring to the JgdPz 38.

In the January 1945 issue of *Nachrichtenblatt der Panzertruppen*, an interesting article describes the basic difficulties of installing and operating the radio system

in the fighting tanks with the limited space available. The company commander vehicles with their expanded equipment were particularly affected.

A JgdPz 38, in service with PzBrig 106 Feldherrnhalle, has been dug-in and effectively camouflaged by the crew. The brigade was established with three PzKpfw V Panther companies.

Inside the company commander's *Jagdpanzer*.

The company is in heavy action. The enemy has broken our line, so we must combine with the escort grenadier squad and the infantry. Here, it depends on the commander issuing clear and careful orders to his platoons while retaining close cooperation with the grenadiers. In addition, the (superior) battalion often wants to have short reports, which in many cases also form the first reports of the battle situation for the InfDiv.

Often the company commander will then want a fifth man for his *Befehlsjäger*. However, there is no room for him in a tank destroyer. In the JgdPz 38 or JgdPz IV, the four-man crew is a cohesive team that has practised and previously fought together. The following suggestions are made in this regard:

1.) The most important task of the lead radio operator is to maintain contact with the battalion. He is dependent on the Fu 8 and is not involved in the on-board communication.

Above: A *Gauleiter* (district leader) from the local Nazi party delivers a speech at a swearing-in ceremony for a recently formed JgdPz 38 unit.

Right: Crew space in the interior of a JgdPz 38 was very limited; even the commander's hatch extended into the engine compartment. Note the three *Pilz* (mushroom) ventilators on the superstructure roof.

2.) The company commander is supposed to lead rather than shoot. But if he has to use his gun, then the lead *Funker* [radio operator] must become the *Laderschütz* [loader]. He switches off the Fu 8, after informing the battalion as to how long he will be off air, and connects his microphone and headphones to the on-board intercom. The battalion staff cannot then reach the tank destroyer company by radio for 15 minutes. The battalion is on continuous reception.

3.) The lead radio operator cannot therefore operate the Fu 5 and the on-board intercom. In the JgdPz IV, the company commander has to take over this task, as this equipment is within his reach and only a few easy-to-learn movements are necessary. In the JgdPz 38, the *Richtschütz* [gunner] is called upon for this task. When the gun is firing, the radio operator becomes the loader and takes over the operation of the Fu 5. This change of tasks has to be practised frequently until the crew has become a well-coordinated 'command group'.

4.) The lead radio operator is the most important assistant to the company commander; he must be able to think along with him, but also be able to act and work independently. That is why this man must be selected with special care.

5.) If the company commander needs to relieve the lead radio operator, the gunner is also trained as a scrambler. He then helps to encrypt and decrypt coded messages. It is therefore possible for the company commander to manage all tasks with his

Any hit from a weapon heavier than an anti-tank rifle would inevitably lead to the loss of a tank. Here, one has been hit by a tank or anti-tank shell, detonating the ammunition and ripping apart the superstructure.

Above: A JgdPz 38 from the production batch issued to front-line units in October 1944. The vehicle left the factory painted in three-colour *Licht-und-Schlatten Tarnung* (light-and-shade camouflage), but the crew has applied foliage to improve concealment in an ambush position.

Right: A JgdPz 38 finished in the camouflage scheme specifically created for fighting in the southern region of the Soviet Union. Note the black bars adjacent to the driver's vision slot, painted on to confuse enemy anti-tank gunners.

When deployed for street-to-street fighting, as here in Prague, it was essential for a JgdPz 38 to be supported by infantry to prevent the enemy from attacking the vulnerable side armour.

four-man crew, the division of duties just has to be clearly defined. Therefore, it should be noted:

a.) The lead radio operator primarily mans the Fu 8; in exceptional cases, he will become the loader.

b.) In JgdPz IV, the lead radio operator mans the Fu 5 and the on-board intercom. In JgdPz 38, the gunner is employed for this purpose; during firing, he is relieved by the radio operator.

c.) The battalion cannot reach the company for a limited time during the firing of the command tank.

d.) Special care must be taken in selection and training of the lead radio operator.

This is an example of the limits of the technology of 1944. The radio equipment took up a large amount of space in the already cramped confines of a tank destroyer. In the JgdPz IV, and even more so in the JgdPz 38, the loader and the gunner had to be trained to be competent radio operators.

It must be clear that the vehicles of the assault artillery were also affected to the same extent. The space required for the radio equipment was basically identical, even if devices were installed that operated in a different frequency range.

Under the impression of the difficult situation in the East, many units were

Although this early production JgdPz 38 was lost in Prague as the battle for the city continued into Spring 1945, it remains fitted with the *Winterketten* (winter tracks).

put together at the end of 1944 that did not correspond to the usual forms of organization. Improvisation was now the order of the day.

These included the *Heeres-Panzerjagd-Abteilung* (H PzJgdAbt) 1 to 6 (note the changed designation), which were formed in December 1944 and January 1945. At first, they had confusingly mixed equipment, as evidenced by a telex dated 24 March 1945:

> Attached to the 3.Panzer Army are: H PzJgdAbt 1, H PzJagdAbt 5 and H PzJagdAbt 6. The H PzJagdAbt 5, last attached to *Korpsstruppe* [unit at corps level] von Tettau, must be considered destroyed. The last remnants (some 70 men, two motorcycles, two cars and four trucks) have been absorbed into H PzJagdAbt 1 and H PzJagdAbt 6. It is currently still operational:
>
> H PzJgdAbt 1
> Six JgdPz 38 [*Hetzer*]: three combat-ready, two in short repair, one in long repair.
> Four StuG III L/48: all combat-ready
> 12 StuG IV: ten combat-ready, two in long repair.

H PzJgdAbt 6
17 JgdPz 38 [*Hetzer*]: six combat-ready, two in short repair, nine in long repair.

In order to create combat-ready units, the PzAOK requests:

H PzJgdAbt 6 to be expanded as follows:
AbtStab, 1.Kp JgdPz 38 [*Hetzer*], 2.Kp (StuG IV) and a supply company.

For this purpose, H PzJagdAbt 1 must provide the following:

- 12 StuG IV to PzJgdAbt 6
- Six JgdPz 38 [*Hetzer*] to 5.JgDiv
- Four StuG III L/48 to H StuGBrig 184

H PzJgdAbt 1 (with staff, staff company and three battle groups) is placed at the disposal of the GenInsp d PzTrp for refreshment.

The shape of the gun mantlet and the steel casting for the driver's vision device identifies this as an early production JgdPz 38. From December 1944, the casting was replaced by a simple slot, protected by a rain shield.

In the turmoil of the retreat, these units deployed at army troop levels were quickly worn down or decisively weakened. Despite all the problems, orders

This JgdPz 38 was abandoned by its crew in the ruins of a village, captured by Allied forces, as their advance continued into Germany. (Getty)

SMRT NĚMECKÝM VRAHŮM

Czechoslovak partisans have painted an anti-occupation forces slogan, 'Death to the German Murderers', on the side of a captured JgdPz 38. Also, they have removed the 7.5cm PaK 39 and covered the aperture with steel plates, leaving a slot for an MG 42. Note the improvized protective shield and StG 44 behind and on the roof.

were issued to refresh what remained of the units.

On 30 March 1945, the GenInsp d PzTrp ordered the refreshment of H PzJagdAbt 1 at the Milowitz military training area. The structure is interesting:

- Staff with two JgdPz 38 and two armoured half-tracks.
- Two tank destroyer companies, each with ten JgdPz 38.
- Two escort grenadier platoons.
- One PzAufklKp with 16 SdKfz 250 or SdKfz 251.
- One supply company.

Despite the fact that the unit was only poorly equipped with *Hetzer* tank destroyers, a *Panzer-Aufklärungs-Kompanie* (PzAufklKp – armoured reconnaissance company) was assigned to the unit in accordance with organization table KStN 1162 'c' (as a non-binding guide), and each tank destroyer company received escort platoons. The supply of the necessary wheeled vehicles proved difficult; workshop vehicles for the maintenance services could only be supplied at a late stage or not at all. This jeopardized the achievement of full operational readiness.

This exceptionally powerful equipment indicated the need for flexibly deployable, fast units, which were to inflict decisive damage on the superior advancing Russian tank units by employing hit-and-run tactics.

Further Development

In order to be able to guarantee JgdPz and StuG the necessary support of infantry forces in winter, the production of simple sledges was requested. Despite extensive tests in the Austrian Alps, nothing is known about the use of these aids.

During 1944, the JgdPz 38 served as the base for a series of further developments. The 7.5cm PaK 39 was to be replaced by a recoilless weapon. Also, at the end of the war, the introduction of a powerful 180hp Tatra eight-cylinder diesel engine was imminent.

In reality, the introduction of a completely new development was planned. Thanks to an enlarged hull, the *Jagdpanzer* 38 D had suffecient room to carry the 7.5cm KwK 42 L/70, as mounted in the PzKpfw V Panther, also in a recoilless mounting. Based on this chassis, new reconnaissance vehicles were projected, armed with a 2cm KwK 38 in a *Hängelafette* (suspended mounting) 38 and the 7.5cm K 51 (L/24). A prototype of a *Flakpanzer*, mounting two 3cm MK 103 cannons and known as the *Kugelblitz* (ball lightning), had also been produced and was undergoing trials. The end of the war prevented the realization of these plans.

On 23 March 1945, Albert Speer wrote to several officials from the army and the HWa:

> The Führer wishes the following vehicles and weapons to be presented to him in accordance with my proposals made towards the middle of April:
>
> 1.) JgdPz 38t with eight-cylinder Tatra diesel engine and fixed 7.5cm L/48 gun
> 2.) JgdPz 38D with 12-cylinder Tatra diesel engine and fixed 7.5cm L/70 gun
> 3.) *Elefant* 21cm on *Hummel* chassis
> 4.) *Elefant* 30.5cm
> 5.) Panther with 8.8cm KwK 44 L/70

All the armoured vehicles mentioned above were mere pipe dreams at the time. The compliant way in which the highly intelligent Speer played along with the game of the increasingly insane German leader, is disturbing.

Jagdtiger 7

It can come as no surprise that the PzKpfw VI Ausf B – known as the *Königstiger* (King Tiger) – was also to serve as the basis for a heavy assault gun. This project was already decided upon during the development phase of the successor to the PzKpfw VI Ausf E Tiger in spring 1943, and work soon began.

The decision-making authority for such development projects and their supervision lay with the HWa. While this office was still working independently before the outbreak of the war, by 1943 other agencies and individuals were also involved. Without really having understood the tactical requirements (and also the logistical consequences) of a modern armoured vehicle, Hitler now also interfered more often in the development of new tanks. In doing so, he set technical benchmarks arbitrarily and lost himself in detail during the many armament discussions. Perhaps impressed by the heavy Russian tanks, Hitler was uncompromising in his demands for the reinforcement of armaments and armour protection, explicitly at the expense of mobility. Frequent false or exaggerated reports from the *Fremde Heere: Ost* (foreign armies: East) office encouraged this development. According to prisoner interrogations, the introduction of super-heavy multi-turret tanks (weight class over 100,000kg) was expected in the East, but all these reports were false.

In January 1943, for example, the Führer supported efforts to increase the frontal armour on the Panther from 80mm to 100mm, and to extend the already highly effective 7.5cm KwK 42 L/70 gun to the exorbitant barrel length of L/100; all without regard to possible negative effects. The increasingly vitriolic German leader prevented open criticism, and the number of acolytes in the round of the *Rüstungsbesprechungen* (armament meetings) was accordingly large. One particularly well-known supporter was Ferdinand Porsche. During the competition for the production contract for the Tiger heavy tank, the eccentric engineer lost out, although Hitler preferred his design to that of

Opposite: 23 May 1945: Two *Jagdtiger* from s PzJgAbt 653, abandoned in the town of Neustadt, near Mannheim. Note the *Fliegerbesuchussgerät* (anti-aircraft mounting) for a 7.92mm machine gun on the engine cover plate.

One of the first *Jagdtiger* during trials in May 1944. The vehicle is fitted with Henschel-type running gear originally designed for the VK 4501, which became the PzKpfw VI Ausf E Tiger.

Henschel. In 1942, however, the HWa was still able to prevail.

In order to make the best possible use of the 100 Porsche-designed hulls already built at the time (1942), a first heavily armoured assault gun was created after extensive modifications. When the *Ferdinand* went into action a few months later during the battle for the Kursk salient (where it revealed its numerous conceptual and mechanical shortcomings), work was already underway on a successor.

The megalomania that had begun was to lead to even heavier tank projects. Thanks to his influence on Hitler, Porsche was able to push through his *Mäuschen* (little mouse); a super tank which was to weigh 180,000kg and be fitted with armour up to 220mm thick and armed with a 12.8cm KwK 44 L/55.

When the PzKpfw VI Ausf B heavy tank went into series production in 1944, it was probably the most powerfully armed and armoured tank of World War II due to its heavy armour (150mm front) and the outstandingly powerful 8.8cm KwK 43 gun. However, this positive assessment is purely theoretical. The significantly increased weight brought serious disadvantages. The tactical mobility of the heavy tank was correspondingly weak, and the same applied to logistics. For railway transport, dedicated tracks (similar to those on the PzKpfw VI Ausf E Tiger) had to be fitted in order to comply with the loading restrictions of a *Sechsachsiger-Flachwagen* (SSyms – six-axle flatcar) railway wagon. This necessitated time-consuming work before the missions. The problems associated with this were certainly foreseeable at the start of production.

Like the *Ferdinand*, the *schwere Sturmgeschütz* (s StuG – heavy assault gun) on the chassis of the PzKpfw VI Ausf B was designed as a more powerful successor to the previous StuG. Initially, the heavy assault gun was to serve as

a support weapon for an infantry attack, so it seemed logical to place it under the command of the artillery.

However, any hopes the *General der Artillerie* had were once again soon dashed. As in the case of the *Ferdinand*, Guderian was to ensure that the new weapon was assigned to 'his' branch of the army, the *Panzertruppe*, as a *Jagdpanzer*. Soon the designation *Jagdtiger* became established.

The heavy assault gun was of conventional construction. A very large casemate superstructure was positioned on top of the PzKpfw VI Ausf B hull, mounted almost centrally and further back than on the *Jagdpanther*. This measure was presumably intended to reduce front-heaviness, which was to be expected due to the weight of the gun and front armour. Since the gun was now mounted further back, the hull had to be extended by 30cm.

The drive components were basically taken over unchanged from the PzKpfw VI Ausf B. However, the increased weight, 75,000kg instead of about 70,000kg for the main battle tank, pushed the engine to its power limits. The Maybach HL 230 P30 delivered a maximum of 700hp. The highly maneuverable

Late summer, 1943: Hitler and the army general staff visit Kummersdorf to inspect a wooden mock-up of the *Jagdtiger* (that of the *Jagdpanther* is in the background). In the foreground is an Italian-built Ansaldo P (*pesante* – heavy) 26/40 *carro armato* (armoured vehicle) mounting an Ansaldo 75mm L/34 gun.

Jagdpanther used the same engine, but it was 30,000kg lighter.

In addition to the improved mobility, the individual components were subjected to significantly lower stress, which made the engine and transmission more reliable.

A well-known weak point on all German tanks were the final drive units. In the case of heavy side loadings, the internal gears used could be easily damaged, potentially leading to the tank becoming immobilized and a possible total loss. During the early phase of the war, when the *Panzertruppe* could still carry out successful offensive operations and the significantly lower-weight PzKpfw III

The first 12 *Jagdtiger* produced had Porsche running gears – two 70cm diameter running wheels were each mounted on four bogies attached to longitudinal torsions bars. Although more cost-effective to manufacture, the suspension caused the vehicle to rock uncontrollably when in motion.

and PzKpfw IV were in use, recoveries could still be successfully made, even under enemy fire.

With the introduction of the heavier PzKpfw VI Ausf B and PzKpfw V Panther tanks, this was to change. The SdKfz 9 heavy half-track tractor was the standard recovery vehicle but it was no longer sufficiently powerful. In addition, the production of this valuable piece of equipment could not keep up with demand. The undoubtedly powerful *Bergepanther* could not haul the weight of the *Königstiger* or *Jagdtiger* without risking mechanical damage.

The *Jagdtiger* was fitted with a Maybach Olvar semi-automatic (pre-selector) gearbox, which proved to be more reliable and simpler to operate, even for an inexperienced driver. In contrast, the manual clutch and gearbox fitted in the *Jagdpanther* required a driver to be well trained in order to avoid damage.

The *Jagdtiger* was armed with a 12.8cm PaK 80 L/44, which had been designed to engage and defeat heavily armoured enemy tanks, fortified gun emplacements and also bunkers at ranges of up to 3,000m with high-explosive (HE) ammunition. At the same time, the heavy armour was intended to make the vehicle immune to enemy fire.

The gun was developed from the 12.8cm FlaK 40 L/61, which had been in service since 1941. Just a year later, the first land combat variant became available and was mounted on a tracked chassis, the 12.8cm K 40 L/61 PzSfl V *Sturer Emil* (Stubborn Emil). Only two of these vehicles, built on a lengthened Henschel-designed VK 3001 chassis, were delivered. Although originally designed as a dedicated *Schartenbrecher*, they were mainly used as tank destroyers because of their powerful gun. Both were lost during the advance on Stalingrad.

The 12.8cm PaK 80 L/55 (sometimes known as the PaK 44) was a further development of this weapon and was supposed to be consistently able to destroy any enemy tank at even longer range. The official armour piercing table indicates a maximum range of 3,500m, but it could penetrate 155mm of armour at 3,000m. This weapon was also the planned armament for the Porsche-designed PzKpfw *Maus* (mouse), the production of which was ordered in 1943. Due to the war situation, the plan was realized.

Essentially, two types of shell were introduced for the weapon mounted in the *Jagdtiger*: the high-explosive 12.8cm SprGr, which weighed 51.8kg (28kg projectile, 23.8kg propellant charge) and the PzGr 43, a conventional armour-piercing projectile with steel cap and ballistic cover, which weighed approximately the same but was slightly shorter. A total of 40 rounds were carried inside the vehicle.

There was a plan to introduce a discard sabot-type projectile (APDS) for the 12.8cm PaK 80, which promised significantly better armour penetration due to its higher material density. However, the muzzle brake on the weapon was not suitable for firing this ammunition.

The old 12.8cm K 40 L/61 and the rifled 12.8cm K 81 L/61 in service with the field artillery, on the other hand, had different types of muzzle brake. Sabot rounds were not introduced until the end of the war.

For self-defence, a 7.92mm MG 34 was fitted in the front of the hull, and two 9mm MP40 were carried in the fighting compartment. For anti-aircraft defence, a 7.92mm MG 42 could be mounted at the rear on the engine deck.

The armour was substantial. The partly surface-hardened rolled steel

reached 150mm at the hull, while the massive casemate superstructure was an even thicker 250mm. On the sides and rear, however, it was 80mm.

In late autumn 1943, Nibelungenwerk in St Valentin, Austria, had received the production order for the *Jagdtiger*. Even before the start of production, Porsche was to intervene again. The visionary engineer suggested to the Führer that the complex interleaved *Schachtellaufwerk* running gear of the PzKpfw VI Ausf B, which had 16 torsion bars, be replaced by a much less complex eight-wheel running gear with external suspension. A running gear of this type was already used on the *Ferdinand*. The time needed for machining the hull could be reduced from 360hrs to 140hrs. This potential saving convinced Hitler, a self-proclaimed expert, who finally ordered the HWa to implement the change.

In February 1944, one *Jagdtiger* with the Porsche running gear and another with the original Henschel type were ready for testing. Although these tests were carried out in a hurry, they did show that the Porsche running gear was inferior to that of the original PzKpfw VI Ausf B. Initially, the two-piece 80cm track used on the *Ferdinand* was held responsible for the problem and 64cm-wide

Production of the *Jagdtiger* was carried out at Nibelungenwerk in St Valentin, Austria, while the company continued to manufacture the PzKpfw IV.

Above: The first *Jagdtiger,* seen here on trials at the Kummersdorf proving grounds. The vehicle is fitted with narrow *Verladekette* (transport tracks) for railway transport. Note the six pieces of standard combat-type wide track carried on the side of the superstructure.

Right: A coating of Zimmerit anti-magnetic paste was applied to all surfaces, but only up to a level of 2.5m. A travelling cradle was fitted to support the heavy barrel of the 12.8cm PaK 44 L/55.

track was fitted as an experiment, but this did not solve the problem.

Henschel prevailed once again, and the original running gear was finally selected for series production.

During the necessary conversion work at Nibelungenwerk, another nine *Jagdtiger* were produced with Porsche running gear before the change could take effect. Since the facility was simultaneously instructed to increase production of the PzKpfw IV to at least 300 vehicles per month, the start-up of the *Jagdtiger* was further delayed.

The first three *Jagdtiger* were accepted in July 1944 but, by the end of November, only 29 of the type had been completed. In December, a further 20 followed, then the monthly output dropped again, resulting in a total of 85 being delivered. Regardless of all the problems experienced during production, the Gen Insp d PzTrp still demanded much heavier combat vehicles in 1944, in line with the wishes of his Fuhrer:

The following further developments are required by the GenInsp d PzTrp:

a) Super heavy tank destroyers

A *Jagdtiger* in the village of Obernephen, March 1945: The tank destroyer was one of four from 2.Zg, 1.Kp, s PzJgAbt 512, sent in an attempt to halt US Army armoured units that had crossed the Rhine at Remagen. This vehicle was immobilized after being hit by a stray *Panzerfaust* (tank fist) anti-tank grenade. The other three were halted by either mechanical failure or lack of fuel.

Gliederung der schw. Pz

Kommandeur: Major Grillenberger

Stabsk

Panzer-Fla-Zug

2. Halbzug
3,7cm Fla   2cm Fla-Vierl.

1. Halbzug
3,7cm Fla   2cm Fla-Vierl.

Fliegerabwehrzug

2cm Fla-Vierl. auf Sfl.

Erkunder- u

m. P

3. Kompanie
Führer: Oblt. Kretschmer

Gruppe Führer

Jagdtiger

3. Zug

Jagdtiger

2. Zug

Jagdtiger

1. Zug

Jagdtiger

2. Kompa

Gruppe Führer

3. Zug

Jagdtiger

2. Zu

Versorgung

Berg

Verwaltungsstaffel	Munitionsstaffel	Betriebsstoffstaffel	Bergegruppe	
			Bergepanzer „Panther"	

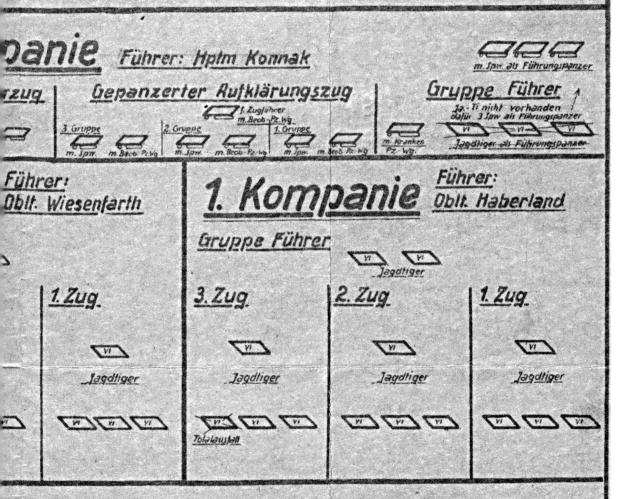

äger - Abteilung 653

Adjutant: Oblt. Scherer

The organizational structure of
Jagdtiger-equipped s PzJgAbt 653.

panie   Führer: Hptm Konnak

m. Spw. als Führungspanzer

zug.   Gepanzerter Aufklärungszug

Gruppe Führer

Ja.-Ti nicht vorhanden
dafür 3 Spw als Führungspanzer

1. Zugführer
m.Beob-Pz.Wg.

3. Gruppe   2. Gruppe   1. Gruppe

m. Spw.   m.Beob-Pz.Wg.   m.Spw.   m.Beob-Pz.Wg.   m.Spw.   m.Beob-Pz.Wg.

m. Kranken
Pz.-Wg.

Jagdtiger als Führungspanzer

Führer:
Oblt. Wiesenfarth

1. Kompanie

Führer:
Oblt. Haberland

Gruppe Führer

Jagdtiger

1. Zug.   3. Zug.   2. Zug.   1. Zug.

Jagdtiger   *Jagdtiger*   *Jagdtiger*   *Jagdtiger*

Totalausfall

ompanie   Führer: Hptm. Ulbricht

J-Staffel
für Räder-Kfz.

Sani-Staffel   Gruppe Führer

Pz-J-Gruppen

nicht
vorhand

rgepanzer „Panther"   3. Pz.J-Gr.   2. Pz.J-Gr.   1.Pz.J-Gr.

15cm L/63, barrel length 10m
17cm L/53, barrel length 10m
Penetration: 200mm at 4,000m range.

These projects were no longer to take place.

The few *Jagdtiger* available were assigned to s PzJgAbt 653, a heavy tank destroyer battalion at army troop level, as focal point weapons. This decision was probably based on the fact that this battalion had been in action since the beginning of 1943 in Russia, with the heavy tank destroyer *Ferdinand*. Despite large numbers of enemy tanks being destroyed in the central and southern sections of the Eastern Front, this heavy vehicle could hardly be called a successful development. The mission in Italy finally turned into a complete fiasco and the few surviving *Ferdinand* were then merged into an independent company that was annihilated in the battle to hold Berlin.

The s PzJgAbt 653 was set up at the same time as other heavy units in accordance with KStN 1149. Due to the assumed high combat effectiveness and the unique nature of the *Jagdtiger*, s PzJgAbt 653 was generously equipped with support vehicles, deviating from the standard organizational structure.

Combat in Lorraine, January 1945: Engineers in s PzJgAbt 653 struggle to fit wide *Gefechtskette* (combat tracks) as snow falls. This was a necessary but time-consuming task after rail transport and often required the use of a heavy half-track tractor.

According to the plan, the battalion was assigned 45 *Jagdtiger* in three companies. Since the total number was too small, the staff company did not receive any command vehicles. Instead, it was issued with SdKfz 251/3 *Funkwagen* (radio vehicle) armoured half-track carriers.

The armoured reconnaissance platoon was equipped with seven SdKfz 251 *Schützenpanzerwagen* (armoured half-track carrier). Another three medium SdKfz 251/7 *Panzerpionierwagen* (PiPzWg – armoured engineer vehicle) were assigned to the reconnaissance and engineer platoon. Great attention was paid to anti-aircraft defence. The *Flugzeugabwehrkanonen Zug* (FlaKZg – anti-aircraft platoon) was issued with three SdKfz 7/1 2cm FlaK-Vierling 38, while the PzFlaKZg was assigned four armoured 3.7cm FlaK 43 *Möbelwagen* (furniture van) and four 2cm FlaK-Vierling 38 *Wirbelwind*.

The recovery squadron was to be issued with five *Bergepanther*, but only four were delivered. A *Munitions-Staffel* (ammunition squadron), a *Betriebstoff-Staffel* (fuel squadron) and a well-equipped *Instandungsetzungs-Kompanie* (InstKp – workshop company) completed the formation of s PzJgAbt 653.

After the end of the war, a number of *Jagdtiger* were transported to the USA for detailed examination. Here, the 72,000kg vehicle has been loaded on a 75,000kg-capacity *Schwerlasttransporter* (heavy-duty transport) designated *Sonderanhänger* (SdAnh – special purpose trailer) 121, manufactured by Culemeyer, originally for the *Deutsche Bundesbahn* (German State Railways).

A *Jagdtiger* in service with s PzJgAbt 653 has been captured by Allied forces as they advanced into Germany. The vehicle has received a hit that has ricocheted off the 150mm-thick front plate and removed the gun's travelling cradle.

Due to the slow start of production, the re-equipment of s PzJgAbt 653 with *Jagdtiger* was delayed and only 16 vehicles had been delivered by the beginning of December. The remaining time available proved to be too short for the troops to adapt to and train with the new equipment.

Equipped with the supposedly powerful vehicles, s PzJgAbt 653 was to take part in the Battle of the Bulge offensive in the Ardennes but, due to transport problems, only 1.Kp with six *Jagdtiger* was initially loaded and, for unknown reasons, the company was not deployed. However, in mid-December, after the arrival of more heavy tank destroyers, the marching order was given and their deployment to the constantly moving frontlines turned into a disaster: eight *Jagdtiger* were left stranded after mechanical problems. Even when more were delivered during *Unternehmen Nordwind* (Operation *North Wind*), the situation still did not improve. More and more *Jagdtiger* broke down on the roads, with their drive components, such as engines and especially final drives, proving to be too unreliable.

On 4 January 1945, s PzJgAbt 653 was attached to the 17.SS-Division Götz von Berlichingen. A strength report issued by the unit shows that only six vehicles were ready for action. Neither the five important *Bergepanther* nor the PzFlaKZg

with four *Wirbelwind* and four *Möbelwagen* were available. Instead of 120 trucks, only 35 had been issued and, of 13 SdKfz 9 heavy half-track tractors, only two had been delivered. Since neither essential supplies nor the delivery of recovery vehicles was ensured, the division was not operationally effective.

A month later, 22 *Jagdtiger* were reported ready for action and the important anti-aircraft and armoured recovery vehicles, as well as a large number of trucks, had finally arrived.

In his operational assessment, the commander, Major Grillenberger, reported:

Special difficulties:

In addition to the already mentioned fragmentation of the battalion, the maintenance elements in particular have been disproportionately weakened.
There is also the lack of an entire workshop company, including the necessary crane and recovery equipment. Also, spare parts are in short supply.
Regarding recovery and supply, it was only possible to work with repair groups and makeshift equipment. Since the *Jagdtiger* is in service for the first time, damage to the steering, gearbox and final drive units is a regular occurrence. There have

Many *Jagdtiger* were abandoned due to lack of fuel or even a minor mechanical failure. Field engineers appear to have attempted the recovery of this vehicle from 2.Kp, s PzAbt512.

The s PzAbt 512 was formed of three companies, each identified by a letter: X (1.Kp), Y (2.Kp) and Z (3.Kp) followed by a vehicle number. This was completely different to standard German armoured vehicle identifiers.

also been several problems with the 12.8cm gun. The hesitation to remedy defects in items leads to a weakening of morale and a lack of confidence in this otherwise excellent tank. The drivers become anxious at the slightest damage because repair services are inadequate and replacement units are unavailable.

All this will improve abruptly when the order is given by *Heeresgruppe* [HG – Army Group] G for the complete assembly of the battalion in the area south of Landau. Eight to ten days after the assembly, it will be ready for any attack and defensive task. It is urgently necessary to remedy the weaknesses of the steering, gearbox and final drive units, as detailed in the mechanical reports sent to those responsible at high command, otherwise disproportionately high losses are to be expected.

The difficult supply situation contributed to further impairment of the battalion's operational capability. For example; the suspension bogies on those *Jagdtiger* equipped with the Porsche-type running gear had proved to be weak. On 29 March 1945, the HWa reported that replacements were to be delivered by truck from Nibelungenwerk directly to the frontline at Bretten, near Karlsruhe. The vehicle and another carrying final drive units apparently did not arrive and the department was forced to send out a search party to retrieve the urgently needed spare parts; all during the chaos of the last six days of World War II.

On 26 March 1945, an enraged Hitler relieved the commander of *Jagdtiger*-equipped s PzJgAbt 653 from his post by Telex (Teleprinter):

GEHEIM [secret]

The commander of s PzJgAbt 653, Major Grillenberger, has to date not lived up to the expectations placed upon him. The Führer has therefore ordered that Grillenberger be dismissed from the army with immediate effect and be recalled as a *Leutnant*. This order is to be carried out immediately by *Oberkommando* West. *Leutnant* Grillenberger is then to be immediately assigned by GenInsp d PzTrp to a PzDiv in combat with the enemy. This is to be reported in detail by 1 July 1945 or immediately if Grillenberger is wounded.

The battalion, which wasted an insane number of resources compared with other combat units, was never to be deployed in an orderly manner.

May 1945: One of the last *Jagdtiger* to be produced at Nibelungenwerk, St Valentin. The vehicle was deliberately blown up in the factory yard to prevent it being taken intact by advancing Allied forces.

Even front-line deployments became a problem. The damaged transport infrastructure meant that equipment had to be moved by road. Marches of 30km threatened to put excessive strain on the sensitive drive components. Mechanical failures were part of everyday life for German engineers, and all too often it was impossible to salvage the heavy vehicles.

In the final phase of the war, the supply of fuel, ammunition and spare parts could no longer be guaranteed. It is almost certain that the majority of the 85 *Jagdtiger* built did not fall victim to enemy weapons. Rather, the vehicles were destroyed by their crews in hopeless situations. There are no stories of success to be found in the archives.

One of the 12 *Jagdtiger* built with the Porsche running gear. The hull was 30cm longer than that of a PzKpfw VI Ausf B, known as *Königstiger* (King Tiger), resulting in there being in a larger gap between the rearmost running wheel and the idler wheel.

Production of the *Jagdtiger* commenced in July 1944 in small numbers. In December, production reached a peak of 20 vehicles, finally reaching the target stock for a s PzJgAbt. A total of 85 vehicles had probably been delivered by the end of the war.

In the spring of 1945, the end of production appeared imminent when gun mountings were no longer available for the 12.8cm PaK. In order that production of the valuable vehicles could continue, it was decided that the 8.8cm PaK 43/3 was to be installed instead. All *Jagdtiger* delivered after March mounted this gun, as confirmed in a document from the OrgAbt K, dated 29 April 1945:

Forecast tank production in May 1945:
Between 90 and 100 PzKpfw IV, depending on the delivery of missing parts (castings for the gearbox and engines).
17 *Jagdtiger* (8.8cm).

Unfortunately, no photographic evidence of the use of these vehicles exists, not even among the numerous wrecks.

Conclusion

The armour and armament of the *Jagdtiger* were exceptional. However, in tough operations in the built-up areas of northern or small-town southern Germany, it should have become clear that there were serious limitations to the tactical use of such heavy vehicles. It was almost impossible (as with all

Opposite: A *Jagdtiger* from s PzJgAbt 512 X (3.Kp) 7 that has been abandoned in a border village after Germany surrendered on 5 May 1945. Material shortages during production meant that many were delivered without the lifting jack and wooden base plate normally carried on the rear of the vehicle.

Left: A *Jagdtiger* immobilized after a direct hit on the right-hand-side running gear and, as was often the case, it was not possible to recover it for repair. The crew has attempted to destroy the vehicle, but only the heavy gun seems to have been torn out of its mounting by a demolition charge.

Linz, Austria: The remnants of s PzJgAbt 653, including two operational *Jagdtiger,* was attached to HG Ostmark when Germany surrendered.

turretless types) to aim at a moving target because the driver had to make major changes in direction with the entire vehicle. Every steering movement on wet ground stressed the transmission and steering brakes; even a damp meadow could lead to it becoming stuck.

Weighing 76,204kg, the *Jagdtiger* hardly proved to be a successful combat vehicle, being neither a heavy assault gun nor a JgdPz, but more a mobile bunker – a concept that was bound to fail.

However, at the same time, the *Jagdtiger* could not be attacked head-on by any Allied anti-tank gun, which was a comfortable situation for the crew. But this hardly represented the reality of the battlefield. The times when German units could successfully engage the haphazard formations of Red Army tanks at long range in the vast steppes of Russia were over.

The 12.8cm PaK 80 armament was comparable to the Soviet-built 100mm M1944 (BS-3) field gun, the most powerful anti-tank gun of World War II. Although s PzJgAbt 653 documented various kills on the Western Front, the hilly and tree-covered terrain meant that its long effective range could never be fully utilized.

Furthermore, the *Jagdtiger* was not indestructible. There is at least one documented kill by US Army troops using an M1 'Bazooka' rocket-propelled anti-tank weapon, penetrated the side armour and detonated the stowed ammunition, resulting in the complete destruction of the vehicle. This is remarkable because the anti-tank weapon should have failed against the 80mm-thick plate, unless it was fired at a very close range of around 30m.

While the *Jagdtiger* was no easy prey, the huge, slow vehicle presented a very large target. Even if the armour could not be cracked by the mass of Allied weapons at close range, hits on the running gear, or drive or idler sprockets, could immobilize the vehicle. If the heavy tank destroyer could not fight its way free, or no recovery or repair was possible, it had to be blown up by the crew.

The *Panzerwaffe* did not achieve its remarkable successes during the fighting in France, the deserts of North Africa and, later, the vastness of Soviet Union with far superior equipment. The early and undeniably great successes were made possible by thinly armoured and comparatively light, but mechanically simple, tanks. The true decisive factors were the offensive strategy on a large scale and the far superior combat tactics of the German forces.

As the war progressed, Allied and Soviet factories proved capable of manufacturing unimaginable quantities of war supplies, while the German side lacked a comparable capacity. The German response initially consisted of the new PzKpfw V Panther medium and PzKpfw VI Ausf E Tiger heavy tanks. Although these had exceptional combat power, they were mechanically no longer durable in the reality of the battlefield.

While German weapon developers produced remarkable guns and ammunition, the motor industry underperformed. Engines and drive components could not meet the increased requirements. With the lighter tank types PzKpfw III and PzKpfw IV, recovery and maintenance could still be managed, but with Panther, Tiger and heavy self-propelled artillery, the *Panzerwaffe* had reached its limits. The introduction of even heavier types, such as the PzKpfw VI Ausf B *Königstiger* and *Jagdtiger*, made the situation untenable.

Sadly, Major Grillenberger, the commander of s PzJgAbt 653, was held responsible by his supreme commander for the tactical failure of a weapon type that could never fulfil the expectations of its creators.

One of the many German armoured vehicles that awaited collection by Allied recovery teams after the war ended. Although the crew of this *Jagdtiger* were under orders to destroy their vehicle, only the roof panel has disappeared. (NARA)

Weaponry 8

Generaloberst Heinz Guderian, who had been relieved of his post at the end of 1941 after numerous disagreements with Hitler, was ordered back to active service in March 1943. In his position as inspector general of the Panzer troops, he was to use his influence to have the tank destroyer known as the *Jagdpanzer*, since it was essentially a dedicated offensive weapon that would play a vital role in future battles.

Assault guns were originally introduced in direct support of the infantry, and were deployed at army troop level in battalion strength (31 StuG), and assigned to various units when required for attacking focal points on the battlefront.

In 1942, the 7.5cm KwK L/48 *lang*, entered service and would prove essential for the continuing fighting in the Soviet Union and North Africa. The weapon was mounted in tank destroyers as the 7.5cm PaK 40 L/46, in *Panzertruppen* as the 7.5cm KwK 40 and in the assault artillery as the 7.5cm StuK 40. The latter two initially had a calibre length of L/43, but this was increased to L/48 in 1943.

Despite the development of more powerful types, these weapons would remain in service until the end of the war because they represented the backbone of the *Panzertruppe* and other armoured formations.

When installed in assault guns, the 7.5cm StuK 40 proved to be extraordinarily successful in defeating the Soviet T-34 medium and KV heavy tanks, which had superior armour. Their prowess was also recognized by the enemy and, as a result, Red Army tank units were instructed to intercept assault gun units only when they were numerically superior.

After his appointment, Guderian intended to discontinue the production of assault guns in favour of conventional tanks. He justified this decision by saying

Opposite: The 9mm MP 40 was the basic self-defence weapon issued to the crews of all German tanks, assault guns and tank destroyers. Although effective, it had a long, rectangular magazine that held 32 rounds, making it somewhat unwieldy to use.

that tanks were more versatile, but his proposal ultimately proved unfeasible since any interference with production would have resulted in a dangerous shortage – the hard-pressed troops, fighting on the battlefront, needed every available armoured vehicle.

Next, Guderian arranged for part of the assault gun production to be made available to the *Panzertruppe,* and so tank destroyer units of Panzer and PzGren divisions were issued with assault guns instead of self-propelled PaK.

Although this measure could only be partially implemented, a new type of vehicle was born. Consequently, the *neues Sturmgeschütz* (new assault gun), the

Two destroyed T-34 M42 medium tanks. Although effectively armoured, any hit that penetrated the side could ignite the fuel (diesel) tanks and stowed ammunition, resulting in the total destruction of the vehicle. (Getty)

development of which was initiated in 1943 on the chassis of the PzKpfw IV, was to be renamed *Jagdpanzer* IV and armed with a derivative of the formidable 7.5cm StuK 40.

7.5cm PaK 39 L/48

Unlike the StuG, the gun was not mounted on a base fixed in the hull. A new space-saving cast-steel gun mounting was bolted directly on the front plate of the superstructure. Not only did this simplify assembly, it also made it easier to remove the gun for maintenance. A heavy cast-metal mantlet was fitted to

Panzer

Weapon	Barrel Length	Calibre Length	Ammunition	Type	Muzzle Velocity
7.5cm KwK 40 7.5cm StuK 40 7.5cm PaK 39	3,600mm	L/48	PzGr 39 PzGr 40 Gr 38 HL/B Gr 38 HL/C SprGr 34	APCBC APCBC HEAT HEAT HE	820mps 990mps 450mps 450mps 550mps
7.5cm KwK 42 7.5cm PaK 42	5,225mm	L/70	PzGr 39/42 PzGr 40/42 SprGr 42	APCBC APCBC HEAT	935mps 1,120mps 700mps
8.8cm KwK 36	4,930mm	L/56	PzGr 39 PzGr 40 SprGr SpGr 39 (HI)	APCBC HVAP HE HEAT	770mps 950mps 810mps 600mps
8.8cm KwK 43 8.8cm PaK 43/2 8.8cm PaK 43/3	6,300mm	L/71	PzGr 39/43 PzGr 40/43 SprGr 43 SprGr 39 (HI)	APCBC HVAP HE HEAT	1,000mps 1,130mps 750mps 600mps
12.8cm PaK 80	7,020mm	L/55	PzGr 43 PzGr 43 SprGr L/5.0	APC-HE APCBC-HE	880mps 920mps 750mps

Official HWa documer

n Guns

Penetration at 100m	Penetration at 500m	Penetration at 1,000m	Penetration at 1,500m	Penetration at 2,000m
106mm	96mm	82mm	67mm	63mm
143mm	120mm	97mm	77mm	63mm
75mm	75mm	75mm	75 mm	--
100mm	100mm	100mm	100mm	--
--	--	--	--	--
138mm	124mm	111mm	99mm	88mm
194mm	174mm	150mm	127mm	106mm
--	--	--	--	--
120mm	110mm	100mm	91mm	84mm
170mm	155mm	138mm	122mm	110mm
--	--	--	--	--
90mm	90mm	90mm	90mm	90mm
202mm	185mm	165mm	165mm	132mm
237mm	217mm	193mm	193mm	152mm
--	--	--	--	--
90mm	90mm	90mm	90mm	90mm
?	?	?	170mm	?
?	?	?	190mm	?
--	--	--	--	--

es give different data.

protect the weapon, mounting and crew.

The barrel was initially fitted with a double-baffle muzzle brake, but this was omitted as production progressed. This was probably due to the cloud of dust that was stirred up as the gun fired, which impaired target observation, obscured the driver's field of vision and made it easy for the enemy to locate the vehicle. The weapon was given the designation 7.5cm PaK 39 L/48.

The same gun was also used, albeit without a muzzle brake and in a slightly modified form, for the series production of JgdPz 38. The 7.5cm PaK 39 L/48 was a semi-automatic gun and fired *Panzergranet-Patrone* (PzGrPatr – cartridge-type ammunition). The gun barrel, designed as a monobloc, was connected to the breech block by a base flange. The drop-block breech opened shortly before the barrel recoil was finished and the empty cartridge case ejected.

A StuG IV that was lost to the advancing Red Army in January 1945. The open maintenance hatch suggests that the transmission has failed. The vehicle appears to be undamaged and retains a complete set of *Panzerschürzen*.

Although the 7.5cm PaK 39 L/48 was selected for use in a number of later projects, none progressed beyond the project design phase.

Sighting

While the *Turmzielfernrohr* (TZF – turret telescope) 5, which had a magnification of 2.5 at an observation angle of 24 degrees, was installed in the PzKpfw IV, the *Zielenfernrohr* (ZF – periscopic sight) 1a, which had a better magnification (5x) at a smaller angle of eight degrees, was fitted for the StuK 40 and PaK 39. As with the assault guns, a *Scherenfernrohr* (SF – scissors telescope) 14 was installed for the commander. This had a field of view of five degrees at 10x magnification, and provided a good means of observation, especially in ambush positions.

Two Panzer IV/70(V), under the protection of escorting infantry, advance to positions on the *Vaterlandlinie* during the final battles against the Red Army advancing from the east. (Getty)

Ammunition

The 7.5cm PaK 39 used the full range of ammunition available for the 7.5cm KwK 40 and the 7.5cm StuG 40. The ammunition for the 7.5cm PaK 40, which was either used as a towed gun or mounted as a self-propelled gun, had longer and slimmer cartridges. Thus, an alternate use of the PaK 40 ammunition was not possible.

The *Jagdpanther* was armed with an 8.8cm PaK 43/3 L/71 – one of the most powerful anti-tank guns of World War II. The well-sloped 80mm frontal armour proved impenetrable by most Allied anti-tank weapons. However, this changed when Allied forces were issued with vehicles armed with the US-built 90mm Gun M3 or the British OQF 17-Pdr anti-tank gun.

7.5cm PzGrPatr 39

This served as a standard armour-piercing projectile to defeat enemy armour. The steel core was tipped with a cap of softer material to absorb the impact shock. Over this soft cap was another ballistic cap that improved ballistic performance. After the caps had flattened, the core – which carried a small explosive charge – penetrated the armour. The 7.5cm PzGrPatr 39 had a tracer which allowed the *Richtschütze* (gunner) and *Panzerfüher* (tank commander) to

Despite its small size and light (16,000kg) weight, the JgdpPz 38, known to troops in the field as the *Hetzer,* was an effective tank destroyer. Although the 7.5cm PaK 39 could defeat most enemy tanks, it was not suitable for offensive combat.

observe the trajectory. The effectiveness of the PzGr 39 has been described in many documents as being totally adequate, which often made the use of the PzGr 40 unnecessary.

7.5cm PzGrPatr 40

As with the 3.7cm and 5cm tank and anti-tank guns, there was also a special ammunition with a tungsten-carbide HVAP (high-velocity armour piercing) core for the 7.5cm PaK 39 L/48. This ammunition had exceptionally good

penetration at ranges of up to 1,000m, but above this the effect decreased exponentially – a peculiarity of this ammunition. Since tungsten was always in short supply, an order was issued for PzGr 40 rounds to only be used to fire on heavily armoured tanks.

7.5cm PzGrPatr 40 (W)

This type of ammunition was externally identical to the standard PzGrPatr 40. However, the tungsten core was replaced by *Weicheisen* (W – mild steel),

Mannheim, May 1945: US Army examine an undamaged *Jagdtiger* abandoned by s PzJgAbt 653. The vehicle is one of the many taken by the Allies for inspection and remains on display at the Aberdeen Proving Grounds in Harford County, Maryland, USA.

In 1945, the HWa published a graphic to illustrate the superior performance of a JgdPz compared with that of Soviet and Allied types in front-on combat.

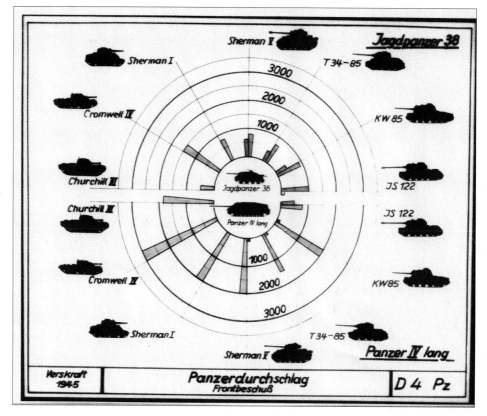

which was in plentiful supply.

According to one official document, this cartridge was only produced as a replacement for the PzGr 40 when tungsten was not available. In this way, the manufacturing facilities producing the high-performance cartridge were not seriously affected.

7.5cm GrPatr 38 HL/B and 7.5cm GrPatr 38 HL/C

The hollow charge projectiles (HEAT) made use of the Munroe effect. The explosive energy of a charge was concentrated in such a way that a jet of metal particles could penetrate even strong armour. The projectiles were effective and inexpensive, but their accuracy was compromised by a slow muzzle velocity and high trajectory. It was possible for penetration performance to be improved from version to version. German documents give the maximum effective range as 1,200m.

7.5cm SprGr-Patrone 34

This was the standard high-explosive round, fitted with *Aufschlagzünder* (AZ – impact fuse) 23. It could be fired with or without the delay.

7.5cm NbGrPatr

This was the standard smoke shell. The use of PzGrPatr 40 (W) and smoke shells was certainly not the rule.

7.5cm PaK 42 L/70

With the development of the new PzKpfw V Panther medium tank, which was to replace the PzKpfw IV, a more powerful armament was also required. Although an improved version of the 8.8cm KwK 36 L/56 mounted in the PzKpfw VI Ausf E Tiger was under development, it was decided to use a 7.5cm gun. As early as 1941, Rheinmetall-Borsig, in Düsseldorf, received an order to develop a 7.5cm tank gun which could penetrate 140mm of armour at ranges of up to 1,000m. The gun, designated the 7.5cm KwK 42 L/70, was available just in time for the start of series production of the PzKpfw V Panther.

The required ballistic performance could only be achieved by increasing the barrel length (calibre length) to its limits. For the gun barrels of the 7.5cm KwK 40, German documents indicate a service life of 2,000 to 3,000 rounds. The durability of a 7.5cm KwK 42 L/70 barrel is identical according to the same source. The 8.8cm KwK 36, which was created from an anti-aircraft gun, lasted an average of 6,000 rounds.

The *schwerer Panzerjäger* (s PzJg - heavy tank destroyer) *Ferdinand* (later *Elefant*) was one of the first armoured vehicles to mount the 8.8cm PaK 43/2. For an unknown reason, the type was initially delivered without a self-defence machine gun.

The first production batch of s PzJg *Ferdinand* ready for delivery to front-line units from the manufacturer Nibelungenwerk, St Valentin, Austria.

Due to lack of space, the JgdPz IV could not be fitted with an armoured ball mounting for a self-defence machine gun. However, an MG42 carried as a defensive weapon could be fired through a gun port.

In 1943, the 7.5cm KwK 42 L/70 was modified for use in (turretless) tank destroyers, making it conceivable to install it in the projected JgdPz IV.

In 1944, the 7.5cm PaK 42 L/70 entered production and utilized the same method of mounting as that used for the 7.5cm PaK 39 L/48. Much like the PaK 39, the Pak 42 also was not fitted with a muzzle brake. However, while the recoil of the PaK 39 was around 48cm, that of the PaK 42 was some 44cm.

Sighting

The *Jagdpanther* was initially fitted with the TZF 12, a telescopic binocular which meant that a gunner had to have a good stereoscopic perception. Since this optic was also difficult and expensive to manufacture, it was soon to be replaced by a monocular version, the TZF 12a. This was almost similar in performance to the TZF 5 fitted in the PzKpfw IV. However, the magnification could be switched from 2.5x to 5x and it had an observation angle of 28 degrees. The new 7.5cm PaK 42 was also fitted with a periscope as used on *Selbstfahrlafette* (Sfl – self-propelled gun) ZF1a). An SF 14 scissors telescope was fitted for the commander.

Ammunition

When developing the ammunition for the 7.5cm PaK 42, the tried and tested projectiles for the 7.5cm L/48 gun were used. The amount of propellant was, however, increased by more than 50 percent, which meant that the cartridges were considerably longer and heavier, making them more difficult to handle.

Since the weapon was mainly intended to be used to fight armoured targets, only three types of ammunition were introduced. The 7.5cm SprGrPatr served as a high-explosive projectile to engage soft or semi-hard targets. The 7.5cm PzGrPatr 39/42 was the standard armour-piercing projectile. The 7.5cm PzGrPatr 40/42, a hard-core projectile, was also available. Apparently, production of the PzGr 40 began and ended in 1943, after which only existing stocks were used. Many field reports indicate that the performance of the PzGr 39 was totally sufficient and, subsequently, no shaped charge projectiles were introduced, and neither were smoke shells.

The 7.5cm PaK 42 was to be installed in the JgdPz IV. The designation was changed to Panzer IV/70 (V) for the variant built by VOMAG and Panzer IV/70 (A) for those produced in Austria by Nibelungenwerk.

The massive breech of the 12.8cm PaK 80 mounted in the *Jagdtiger*. Ammunition was stored in racks on the sides of the fighting compartment and under the gun mounting.

Both the PzKpfw III and PzKpfw IV had a ball-mounted self-defence machine gun fitted in the front plate of the superstructure. The preferred weapon was a 7.92mm MG 34 fitted with an armoured sleeve, but on many occasions the standard type had to be used.

8.8cm PaK 43

In parallel to the development of the 7.5cm PaK 42, a new 8.8cm anti-tank gun, based on the 8.8cm FlaK 41, which had an extraordinary ballistic performance, was ordered. In comparison with an 8.8cm KwK 36 L/56, the armour penetration improved by some 60 percent. Again, this was achieved by lengthening the barrel from 4,930mm (KwK 36) to 6,300mm, resulting in a calibre length of L/71.

The weapon was initially to be fitted with a two-piece barrel as the 8.8cm PaK 43/41 but, after a short time, a new, improved variant, fitted with a simplified gun cradle assembly, entered production. Designated as the 8.8cm PaK 43 L/71, it had a two-piece barrel and an improved gun carriage.

Even when the gun was at the development stage, German military planners had already decided to mount the weapon in various armoured vehicles.

The self-propelled gun *Hornisse* – later *Nashorn* – mounted the 8.8cm PaK 43/1, a development of the PaK 43/41.

The heavy tank destroyer *Ferdinand* (later *Elefant*) mounted the 8.8cm PaK 43/42, a special variant of the 8.8cm PaK 43 with a monobloc gun barrel. Initially, the 8.8cm PaK 43/3 used in the *Jagdpanther* also had this monobloc gun barrel but, in May 1944, a two-piece type was introduced to simplify production.

The successor to the PzKpfw VI Ausf E Tiger, the even heavier Ausf B *Königstiger*, was originally also fitted with the 8.8cm KwK 43 with a monobloc barrel, and then a two-piece type as production continued.

Sighting

As with the other JgdPz, a ZF1a (Sfl) was installed in the *Jagdpanther* and the *Ferdinand*, as was the SF 14 scissors telescope.

Ammunition

The basic ammunition design for the 8.8cm PaK 43/1 L/71 was similar to that for the 8.8cm FlaK 41. The cartridges were significantly enlarged in comparison with those for the 8.8cm KwK 36 L/56, as mounted in the PzKpfw VI Ausf E Tiger.

This weapon was to be primarily used to fight tanks, and three types of ammunition were available:

- 8.8cm SprGrPatr
- 8.8cm PzGrPatr 39-1/42
- 8.8cm PzGrPatr 40/42

The 8.8cm SprGrPatr served as the standard high-explosive shell. The standard armour-piercing projectile was the 8.8cm PzGrPatr 39-1/42. There was also a tungsten-core type which was designated the 8.8cm PzGrPatr 40/42. Unlike with the 8.8cm KwK 36 L/56, no shaped charge ammunition was introduced.

12.8cm PaK 80

As early as 1942, K40, a variant of the 12.8cm FlaK 40, was developed and mounted on a self-propelled gun carriage, but only two were produced. Based on this work, Krupp and Rheinmetall-Borsig went on to develop further 12.8cm types, which were to be introduced as multi-purpose guns. Originally, the plan was to replace the 10cm *schwere Kanone* (s K – heavy gun) 18 of the field artillery with a new flat-trajectory gun, which had a performance totally superior to that of an anti-tank gun. In 1944, two different proposals were put forward – one for a towed 12.8cm gun, mounted on a cruciform carriage, and one for a self-propelled gun. However, neither type went into large-scale production.

Only one variant, the 12.8cm PaK 80, was produced in larger numbers from 1944. It had a monobloc gun barrel and was mounted in a two-piece jacket-type cradle fitted with a recoil brake and pneumatic recuperator. To pivot the upper carriage, trunnions were bolted to the sides of the cradle and the upper carriage was mounted on a base plate bolted to the bottom of the hull.

The recoil brake had to absorb all (some 90cm) of the after-firing recoil. However, for unknown reasons, the PaK 80, unlike the planned field guns, was

From December 1944, a platform was fitted on the engine deck of the *Jagdtiger* to carry a *Fliegerbeschussgerät* (anti-aircraft mounting) for a 7.92mm MG 42, which was used for defence against ground-attack aircraft.

not fitted with a muzzle brake to dissipate some of this force. Presumably this was the reason why the chassis of the PzKpfw VI Ausf B *Königstiger* was extended by 30cm. The massive gun had a hand-operated, horizontally opening, sliding wedge-type breech block.

Sighting

The 12.8cm PaK 80 mounted in the *Jagdtiger* was fitted with a *Winkel-Zielfernrohr* (WZF – periscopic sight) 2/1 for direct aiming. This sight had very high optical

All arms of the *Wehrmacht* were issued with the 27mm Walther *Leuchtpistole* (signal pistol) 42. The smooth-bore weapon was used to fire a wide range of cartridges, including coloured flares, illumination, smoke and even sound signals.

performance, making it particularly suitable for use at dusk and at night.

The WZF had 10x magnification and a field of view of seven degrees. As in other types, it also was fitted with an SF 14.

Ammunition

The weapon fired a two-piece type of ammunition – a Gr was loaded in the breech, followed by a brass-cased propellant charge. While a wider range of ammunition was provided for the those guns intended for field artillery, only two projectiles were available for the 12.8cm PaK 80:

- 12.8cm PzGr 43
- 12.8cm SprGr L/5.0

The 12.8cm PzGr 43 was used to engage armoured targets, while the 12.8cm SprGrL/50 was the standard high-explosive projectile.

The *Nahverteidigungs-waffe* (close-combat weapon) could be rotated 360 degrees and was simple to load and fire.

SECONDARY WEAPONS

Both the StuG and the JgdPz were designed for offensive operations using mounted weapons with very limited traverse and elevation. When breaking through enemy positions, the heavy frontal armour was virtually impervious but, if the vehicle was halted, enemy close-combat teams could attack the weaker side armour. Consequently, it was ordered that whenever any of the type were in combat, they were to be protected by *Begleit-Grenadier*. Unfortunately, this could not always be guaranteed.

The most widespread anti-tank weapons in service with the Red Army were the heavy PTRD and PTRS anti-tank rifles, both of which fired a 14.5mm projectile that could penetrate up to 30mm at close range. This made them very dangerous for the early assault guns, but they were less of a menace to a *Jagdpanzer*, which had thicker, sloping armour. Nevertheless, a small risk remained, as the Red Army had an enormous stock of these weapons. Importantly, a 14.5mm projectile could easily damage individual components such as the track, running gear, vents and vision devices. The introduction of 5mm *Panzerschürzen* plates to protect the sides of vehicles was a direct consequence of this threat.

Enemy close-combat teams operating on the battlefield placed explosive charges, mines or even jammed pieces of metal in the running gear. A defence against these forces was essential.

A tank was equipped with self-defence weapons; a coaxial MG in the

The *Nahverteidigungswaffe* was fitted in most German tanks, StugG and JgdPz. The weapon was used to fire either a smoke cartridge for laying a defensive screen or a fragmentation grenade, which was used if the vehicle was attacked by enemy infantry or a close-combat team.

turret, another ball-mounted MG in the front plate and a number of opening pistol ports. However, in an assault gun or a tank destroyer there was simply no space in which to fit these effective weapons. Both the *Jagdpanther* and *Jagdtiger* had a spacious superstructure, allowing a 7.92mm MG 34 to be carried in an armoured ball-type mounting fitted in the front plate.

The JgdPz IV and Panzer IV/70 had large opening appertures at the front, through which a machine gun could be fired. However, these did not offer sufficient protection; shell splinters and well-aimed infantry shots could pass through into the interior, endangering the crew.

As a very small vehicle, the JgdPz 38 had no space for self-defence weapons. The crews of tanks, assault guns and tank hunter/destroyers had a limited number of hand weapons that were suitable for defence. Officers and NCOs were issued with either a 9mm Luger P08 or 9mm Walther P38 pistol, and a 9mm MP 40 was supplied for general use. The crew of a JgdPz 38, for example, was issued with one MP 40, whereas a *Jagdpanther* crew had two.

From the end of 1942, many attempts were made to improve self-defence for the crews of assault guns and tank destroyers, but all the proposals had the same serious disadvantage – the hatches had to be opened, which made the gunner vulnerable to enemy fire. Many casualties had to be accepted in an attempt to protect the vehicle.

The search for a solution to this dilemma was complicated by the fact that German industry lacked capacity and material. From 1944, some solutions were developed and introduced on a limited scale.

Smoke Grenade Launcher

Smoke grenades were available early in the war as a passive means of protecting armoured vehicles. The externally mounted *Nebelkurzenabwurfvorrichtung* (NKAV – smoke grenade launcher) was fitted on tanks and assault guns. Although considered to be effective, they were susceptible to being pre-ignited by infantry fire and shell splinters. This was the reason why the NKAV was dropped in late 1943.

Close-defence Weapon

In 1944, the *Nahverteidigungswaffe* (close-defence weapon) was installed in various battle tanks, assault guns and tank destroyers. Basically, the device was a slanted 90mm diameter tube, fitted in the roof of a turret or superstructure, which could be rotated through 360 degrees. The device was used to fire flares, smoke grenades to screen a vehicle and fragmentation grenades with delay fuses to defeat enemy close-combat teams. But these had to be used with great care so as not to endanger German supporting infantry. It was also possible to fire a *Kampfpistole* (combat pistol) – sometimes referred to as a *Sturmpistole* (assault pistol) – through the open device. From June 1944 onwards, virtually every tank, tank destroyer and assault gun was to be factory-fitted with this close-defence weapon. But there was a problem – it could not be manufactured in the required quantities due to a shortage of materials.

The all-round fire MG 34 was protected by a simple curved gun shield. The weapon could be installed in both the StuG and JgdPz without any modifications.

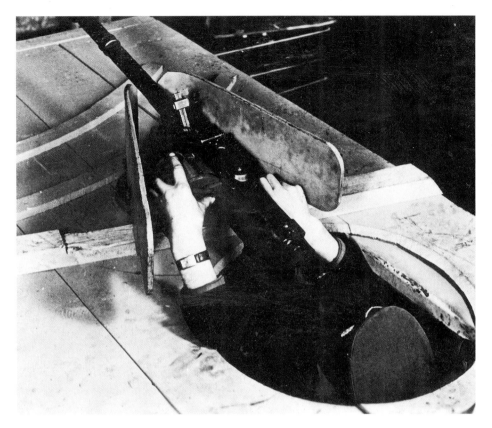

The *Rundum-Feuer Maschinengewehr* (all-round fire machine gun) was a valuable weapon for self-defence. The device rotated through 360 degrees and was operated from inside the vehicle by a system of rods and levers. An observation and aiming periscope was fitted in the roof panel. However, the hatch had to be opened to change a magazine.

Rundum-Feuer MG

In 1942, Daimler-Benz developed a device that allowed a machine gun to be remotely operated of from inside a vehicle. The *Rundum-Feuer Maschinengewehr* (all-round fire machine gun) could be installed in a StuG and JgdPz.

The device, which could rotate through 360 degrees, was mounted on the roof of the superstructure and controlled by levers operated by the loader. The gun, a 7.92m MG 34, was fitted with a *Gurttrommel* (belt drum magazine) containing 50 rounds, and was protected by a curved armoured shield. However, this provided only limited protection for the gunner because he had to open the hatches to reload.

The *Rundum-Feuer* MG was fitted to all production *Hetzer*, as well as a large proportion of the last batches of StuG III and StuG IV manufactured.

A prototype of the JgdPz IV also featured a *Rundum-Feuer* MG, but this effective weapon was not introduced on production vehicles, possibly due to a lack of materials. No further *Jagdpanzer*, apart from a few exceptions, were to receive the close-defence weapon.

After attending a troop trial with StuGBrig 189 in spring 1944, the general of artillery noted that he found the device to be useful and effective.

Allied and Soviet Types 9

Both equipment and operational methods of Allied anti-tank units differed considerably from the German approach.

As in the German army, towed anti-tank weapons were the first to be deployed. These weapons were supplied to both infantry and armoured units.

Anti-tank weapons moved by motor vehicles or horses basically had limited mobility, especially under unfavourable weather conditions or difficult terrain. But mobility soon improved when powerful tracked or half-track tractors began to enter service. However, the rapidly improving armour protection of the tanks at the beginning of the war led to the development of more powerful anti-tank weapons – which in turn were larger and heavier.

Towed anti-tank weapons, despite their limited tactical mobility, could be used well in defensive engagement. However, an enemy breakthrough could easily result in the loss of equipment and gunners. An offensive use of the weapons was hardly possible. The lack of protection for the crew against infantry and artillery fire remained a major problem. The crew was also exposed to the rigours of the climate. The troops were forced to help themselves with improvisations.

The introduction of industrially manufactured self-propelled guns was a first step towards solving these problems. Germany introduced different solutions in large quantities from 1942 onwards. Due to the overall insufficient capability of German industry, chassis from different manufacturers were used, with a corresponding negative impact on the supply of spare parts and maintenance.

In principle, self-propelled guns offered significantly increased mobility and a certain degree of armour protection compared with towed anti-tank weapons. If these weapons were used in a tactically sensible way, they proved themselves to be highly valued asset, especially on the Eastern Front. In total, some 3,000 self-propelled tank destroyers were produced by the Germans.

Opposite: The 76mm Gun Motor Carriage (GMC) M18 Hellcat was purposely designed with 25mm armour to keep it light (17,000kg) and highly mobile.

In 1943, Soviet military planners issued orders for the series production of a self-propelled gun which utilized the chassis of the T-60 light tank and mounted a 76mm M1942 (ZiS-3) divisional gun. The resulting vehicle was designated the SU-76 or SU-76M and, due to a highly efficient centralized armaments industry, some 12,000 had been completed by the end of the war.

Both Great Britain and the USA decided not to introduce a comparable type of weapon in significant numbers. Only one self-propelled gun was developed on

Several 76mm GMC M10 leaving landing craft at Slapton Sands, Sterte Bay, Devon, during one of the rehearsals for the D-Day landings on 6 June 1944. The tank destroyer force went ashore as part of the second wave.

the basis of the M3 half-track. The M3 Gun Motor Carriage (GMC) carried the licensed variant of a French-designed gun, the 75mm M1897A5, and more than 2,000 vehicles were produced. The utility of these vehicles was limited, because the gun lacked firepower and the vehicle lacked effective armour and mobility.

From 1942 onwards, Germany increasingly relied on assault guns, which, as fully armoured vehicles, represented a new type of anti-tank weapon. This concept was then developed further to create the *Jagdpanzer*.

On the left is the prototype of the SU-101 (Uralmarsh-1), designed to replace the smaller SU-100 heavy tank destroyer which entered service towards the end of 1944.

The SU-100 was developed from the SU-85 and mounted a 100mm D-10S (one of the most powerful guns of World War II), which was capable of defeating the heavily armoured PzKpfw VI Ausf B *Königstiger*. The SU-100 remained in front-line service into the 1960s.

Red Army

As many documents show, the Red Army command was very impressed by the German StuG. At times, orders were given not to engage any German unit issued with the type or only to attack if their own forces were heavily outnumbered. It is not known to what extent the StuG influenced the Soviet military planners to initiate the development of a comparable type.

The first Soviet assault gun, the SU-122, appeared in 1943. Based on the T-34, a fixed superstructure was used and mounted a 122mm M1938 (M-30) gun. In parallel to this, the SU-152, armed with a 152mm ML-20S howitzer heavy assault gun, was built on the chassis of the KV-1 tank. Although both types were successfully used to fight German heavy tanks, since they both were armed with an artillery weapon rather than a high velocity anti-tank gun, it is

The M36 was armed with the 90mm Gun M3 which had the power to fight all German tanks, even at long ranges. All US tank destroyers had an open turret, providing no protection from the shrapnel of an air-burst shell. (Getty)

difficult to designate them as tank hunters/killers.

With the availability of the 85mm M1938 (M-30) gun, originally developed as an anti-aircraft gun, there was finally a weapon available that had the range to engage the German Panther and Tiger tanks. The SU-85, the first Soviet tank killer, entered service in 1944 and some 2,700, including the SU-85M, had been delivered by December of that year.

Since the T-34/85 was being delivered to front-line units in increasing numbers from mid-1944, it was decided that the SU-85 was to be re-armed with the much more powerful 100mm D-10S L/56 gun. Delivery of the type,

April 1945: A column of 90mm GMC M36 from the US Army 607th Tank Destroyer Battalion cross a pontoon bridge, assembled by field engineers, over the Saale at Saalfeld, Germany.

designated SU-100, began in 1945 and it is thought that some 2,500 had been produced by the end of the war.

US Army

According to US tank destroyer doctrine, the fight against attacking enemy tanks was reserved for the specialized forces of the tank destroyer battalions. Conventional tanks like the M4 Sherman medium tank, on the other hand, were to accompany the infantry and enable the breakthrough.

After the first experiences with the GMC M3 half-track, it was decided that anti-tank weapons would be installed on light armoured tracked vehicles. Basically, high mobility was required, and so the armament was to be mounted in an open-topped rotatable turret. The first M10 GMC tank destroyers (unofficially known as the 'Wolverine') were available when US forces landed in North Africa. These were built by utilizing the hull of an M4A1 Sherman medium tank fitted with an open turret mounting a 3-inch (76.2mm) Gun M7. However, it quickly became apparent that this weapon was ineffective against the armour on the PzKpfw VI Ausf E Tiger.

As a result, US military planners issued an urgent order for the development of a new type, the GMC M36 mounting a 90mm Gun M3, for delivery to front-line units in 1944. As with the M10, the M36 utilized M4 Sherman components because the type was known to be mechanically reliable.

In addition, the M18 Hellcat was designed and developed as a lightweight, fast and highly manoeuvrable tank destroyer. Uniquely, the M18 was fitted with automatic transmission and had a top speed of 89kph. The type was armed with a long-barrelled 76mm Gun M1, which had a similar performance to the 7.5cm KwK 42 L/ 70 mounted in the PzKpfw V Ausf A Panther.

The US-built M10, M36 and M18 had significantly higher tactical mobility

compared with the German JgdPz, and their mechanical reliability was considerably better. Since their armour was deliberately kept to the minimum in the interest of speed, the US tank destroyers were, in the first instance, deployed for defensive operations. But the majority were kept at a high state of operational readiness for rapid deployment to hot spots on the battlefield.

British Army

The first self-propelled tank destroyer guns did not enter service with British armoured forces until 1942. Initially, an OQF 2-Pdr was carried on a Gun *Portée* light truck, and then a much more powerful type mounting the OQF 6-Pdr followed: the AEC Gun Carrier, Mk I, Deacon, which utilized the four-wheel-drive Matador truck chassis. Both vehicles were used only in the deserts of North Africa and, although the latter was lightly armoured, the OQF 6-Pdr could defeat PzKpfw IV and StuG. The arrival of the PzKpfw VI Ausf E Tiger on the battlefront caused British military planners to accelerate the development of the OQF 17-Pdr anti-tank gun. Fortunately for British forces, a number of pre-production guns had been delivered and were to prove effective at damaging (or defeating) the German heavy tank.

The 76mm GMC M10 was the first specific tank destroyer issued to US forces. The vehicle has been fitted with a Culin hedgerow-cutting device, which was designed to cut through the dense foliage in Normandy.

The 76mm GMC M18 Hellcat was purposely designed with 25mm armour to keep it light (17,000kg) and highly mobile. The type, manufactured by Buick, was the first US tank to have torsion bar suspension and automatic – Detroit 900T Torqmatic – transmission.

August 1944: An M-10 tank destroyer passes through the town of San Casciano, some 15km southwest of Florence, Italy. The vehicle is in service with the 7th Anti-tank Regiment, 2 Division, 2nd New Zealand Expeditionary Force (NZEF). (NARA)

A column of 90mm GMC M36, each with their guns secured in the travelling cradle, advance towards the battlefront. The leading vehicle is towing an ammunition trailer.

When sufficient numbers of the OQF 17-Pdr gun became available, British military planners decided to mount the weapon in the M10 tank destroyer. Those converted were designated as the Achilles IIC. Here, one of the type crosses over a Churchill Ark Mk II submerged in a stream.

In 1943 British forces received, under the Lend-Lease Program, their first tank dedicated tank destroyer: the US-built GMC M10. The type was armed with the 76.2mm gun, which proved to be effective but was not always able to deal with the heavier German tanks.

Aware of the coming Operation *Overlord* (D-Day landings on 6 June 1944), and encouraged by the performance of the OQF 17-Pdr gun, British military planners made the decision to increase production to allow the gun to be mounted in other types. The first to be selected was the GMC M10, which was subsequently re-designated as the 17-Pdr, Self-Propelled, Achilles Mk IIC. The type was mainly issued to units attached to tank forces with less effective armament. By the end of the war, some 1,000 of the original 1,650 vehicles received from the US had been converted.

In order to improve combat mobility, a new type was developed in 1944, utilizing the chassis of a Tank, Infantry, Valentine Mk III. Due to the small size of the donor tank, the turret had to be removed and replaced with an open-top armoured superstructure. The gun, which could be traversed 11 degrees to

each side and elevated between minus 7.5 degrees and plus 15 degrees, was mounted in the fighting compartment and faced to the rear, over the engine deck, so that the overall length of the vehicle was kept as short as possible.

The vehicle, which entered service as the Self-Propelled 17-Pdr Valentine Mk I, Archer, was designed primarily for defensive operations; the unusual layout of the type made it possible to exit a firing position quickly without having to turn the vehicle around. By the end of the war, a total of 655 had been built.

The OQF 17-Pdr was also mounted in the A30 Challenger, Sherman VC (M4A4) Firefly and the Sherman (M4A1) IIC Firefly to improve the firepower of front-line tank units.

Men of the Royal Engineers (RE) work to repair the roadway over a bridge as a column of Achilles tank destroyers prepare to enter Coesfeld before advancing on the city of Münster.

Conclusion

The JgdPz was created to seek and defeat the heavily armoured and more effectively armed Soviet types that were appearing on the battlefront in vast numbers. It was important to German military planners that they utilize the chassis of current types so as not to interrupt production. From 1943, it was imperative that the German war machine received every available tank. The change in priority from the PzKpfw IV to the more powerful PzKpfw V Panther was not possible without a temporary slump in the numbers built. In the last two years of the war, this resulted in a higher proportion of JgdPz and

The Self-Propelled
17-Pdr Valentine Mk 1,
Archer, was designed
to give British forces
fighting in Europe much-
needed extra firepower.
The type utilized a
standard infantry tank
chassis with a OQF
17-Pdr gun, protected
by a rudimentary shield
mounted over the
fighting compartment.
The weapon pointed to
the rear over the engine
bay. Over 600 had been
produced by the end of
the war.

StuG within the total number of German tanks in service.

The absence of a rotatable turret allowed for the installation of a more powerful gun and, within certain limits, the provision of heavier armour. Most types were designed with a low profile, which allowed the vehicle to be easily concealed in a well-camouflaged firing position. The frontal armour, which was superior to that of most comparable enemy tanks, allowed the crew to disengage from a fight with minimal damage.

But the type had a serious disadvantage: the design allowed the main gun a very limited range of traverse. A moving target was difficult to attack, and the driver would have to manoeuvre his vehicle, which in turn overloaded the vulnerable transmission. This was a common fault on all German tracked vehicles.

Ultimately, the tactical skill of the commander and his crew would be the decisive factor in proving the combat value of the tank hunter/destroyer. This would also apply to the crews of Soviet and Allied tank destroyers, although their deployment on the battlefront differed.

The OQF 17-Pdr gun mounted on the Archer could be elevated from minus 7.5 degrees to plus 11 degrees and traverse 11 degrees to the left and right. On 8 February 1945, Allied forces launched Operation *Veritable* but, on 9 February, German forces blew up the gates of the largest Roer dam (followed by many others) to flood the valley and slow the advance.

Index

The assembly hall at the MNH factory in Hannover. All production at the facility ended in March 1945 after a series of heavy raids by Allied bombers.

A line of *Jagdtiger* in the final stages of completion at Nibelungenwerk, St Valentin, Austria.

Acknowledgements

The author evaluated a vast amount of information that was searched for and found in public archives including the Bundesarchiv/Militärarchiv (BAMA), Freiburg, Germany, and the National Archives & Records Administration (NARA), Washington, USA. An invaluable source was the internet-based project for digitizing German documents in the archives of the Russian Federation. Every document found there was carefully evaluated in the context of its historical background and represents a significant portion of the book.

The technical aspects of the tank hunters have been extensively evaluated in the *Panzer Tracts* series of publications produced by the late Thomas Jentz and Hilary L. Doyle, which I recommend for further information. I also used books written by Walter J. Spielberger as a source and inspiration. Other post-war publications were used only to a limited extent.

Firstly, my sincere thanks to Peter Müller, publisher of *History Facts*, a true friend who provided much valuable information and advice.

My gratitude to the following individuals who granted me access to their collections: Florian von Aufseß, Karlheinz Münch, Henry Hoppe and Wolfgang Zimermann.

Thanks to my editor, Jasper Spencer-Smith, that ever-patient gentleman, for his guidance and work on my manuscript and the completed book. Also, thanks to Crispin Goodall for his carefully prepared page layout.

All images in this book are, unless otherwise credited, from the Thomas Anderson Collection.

Bibliography

Doyle, H. & Jentz, T.: *Panzer Tracts*, various editions – Panzer Tracts, Boyds, ML, USA.

Guderian, H.: *Errinen eines Soldaten*, first edition – Kurt Vowinckel Verlag, Heidelberg, Germany.

Jentz, T.: *Die Deutschen Panzertruppen*, Volumes 1 & 2 – Podzun-Pallas Verlag, Eggolshiem, Germany.

Nehring, W.: *Die Geschichte der Deutschen Panzerwaffe 1916 bis 1945* – Motorbuch Verlag, Stuttgart, Germany.